SPUD MAN'S
SPUDS
FOR ALL
SEASONS

SPUD MAN'S

SPUDS FOR ALL SEASONS

SPUD
OF THE BEST SPUD
Garlic Butter
BBQ pulled
JACKET SPUD

SPUD MAN'S

SPUDS FOR ALL SEASONS

SPUDTACULAR WHATEVER THE WEATHER

40 banging seasonal recipes

Harper North

WHEN USING KITCHEN APPLIANCES
PLEASE ALWAYS FOLLOW THE
MANUFACTURER'S INSTRUCTIONS

The author and publishers do not accept any responsibility for any injury or adverse effects that may arise from the use or misuse of the information in this book.

HarperNorth
Windmill Green
24 Mount Street
Manchester M2 3NX

HarperCollins*Publishers*
1 London Bridge Street
London SE1 9GF

www.harpercollins.co.uk

HarperCollins*Publishers*
Macken House,
39/40 Mayor Street Upper
Dublin 1, D01 C9W8, Ireland

First published by
HarperCollins*Publishers* Ltd 2026

1 3 5 7 9 10 8 6 4 2

A catalogue record of this book is available from the British Library

ISBN 978-0-00-883154-7

Photography / Styling / Art Direction:
Natalie Garforth
Food Stylist: Lee-Ann Snyman
Designer: Louise Leffler
Recipe Developer: Heather Thomas

Printed and bound in Latvia by PNB

To all my little spuds
And to Sarah

SPUDCONTENTS

SPUDTACULAR WHATEVER THE WEATHER!

40 BANGING SEASONAL RECIPES

BEING SPUDMAN

You'll know this if you've ever seen my content before – or bought my first book – but my dad was a potato merchant and he supplied pretty much 99 per cent of the potato vendors around the country, partly because he pre-wrapped his spuds in foil, which saved them a lot of time. No one does that anymore. I used to go around with him and deliver them when I was a kid. So I grew up around potatoes. My grandad was a farmer as well. For as long as I can remember, I've been involved in the potato industry.

FOR AS LONG AS I CAN REMEMBER, I'VE BEEN INVOLVED IN THE POTATO INDUSTRY

My dad had supplied the previous owner of my pitch on St Editha's Square, Tamworth for over twenty years before I took it over, which is how I knew about it. I used to eat potatoes here as a kid. At seventeen I was young, carefree and hungry so I thought 'why not give it a go?' I've been in Tamworth since 2003, when I bought the pitch from the previous owner, who was retiring.

I love this spot, next to the church and all the other traders in this beautiful, friendly town. This place was once capital of Mercia, one of three Anglo-Saxon kingdoms, and now it rules the baked spud kingdom. I've been given an Honorary Freedom of the Borough, like some sort of medieval gentleman. It couldn't have happened anywhere but here in Tamworth.

But I also love visiting other places, and I've done a lot of touring this summer. We've been to Burton upon Trent, Biggleswade, Stoke Mandeville, Wrexham, Cleethorpes, Derby – and loads else besides. People have come from far and wide to try our spuds: from Australia, America and Canada. It's the greatest compliment. And loads of the people who turn up have never had a baked potato before, so it's a big responsibility.

I LOVE MY SPOT NEXT TO THE CHURCH AND ALL THE OTHER TRADERS IN BEAUTIFUL, FRIENDLY TAMWORTH

THE WEIRDEST, MOST SURREAL THING I'VE DONE RECENTLY WAS SERVING SPUDS WITH THE QUEEN

But when it comes to the events calendar, there's one that stands above all others: Bloodstock. It's on our doorstep and it's the nicest crowd. They're metalheads. My people. They just eat and eat and eat and eat – absolutely hammer us. I love it. It's a really cool festival and we get looked after brilliantly by the organisers. We also really go above and beyond for them. We have merch made for it. We redesign the trailer.

Spring is my favourite time of year because it's not too hot in that wagon, but it's not cold. I don't feel like an idiot wearing shorts like I do in the winter, but I still refuse to put trousers on. And it's kind of like we've got through that winter period and the summer's coming and I'm all enthusiastic for the events. But we haven't started the events, so I'm not all like worn out yet. But every day is a good day to eat a baked potato.

The weirdest, most surreal thing I've done recently was serving spuds with the Queen to celebrate Meals on Wheels Week. She told me her son, food writer Tom Parker Bowles, had never forgotten the spud I served him when he visited Tamworth in 2024. I was just impressed she knew who I was. She did really well; she's a natural. Getting the butter on, serving the customers – brilliant. What a whirlwind. She served herself a tuna mayonnaise one.

But it isn't always royalty who leave the biggest impressions. I had one customer not so long ago who really sticks in my head. This lovely lady comes up to the front of the trailer, and she orders a potato and told me her story. She made me cry – and I'm sure she won't mind me saying this. She told me it was on her husband's bucket list. I looked around and her husband wasn't there. I just instantly knew what she meant. I grabbed her hand, she started crying and I started crying. It was absolutely the sweetest thing. Mike, you weren't there but we ticked one off your bucket list for you mate. You weren't forgotten.

Of course, for all the emotion this job brings, at its heart it remains a story about one thing: the potato.

Some days I eat more than one spud. I've got to eat at least 300 potatoes a year; at least six in seven days I eat a potato. Though if my doctor's reading this it's less than that because they're high in potassium and that's not good for me.

If I had to eat another type of potato-based food for the rest of my life, it would have to be roasties. Like, really crispy Parmesan, buttery roast potatoes. You know, when they're like herby and Parmesan all over the top and you toss them and they sound like a rock. Yeah, that.

I've got nine kids so baked potatoes are a staple at home. I love lasagna too. We need to do a lasagna baked potato. Somehow. My kids are basic though. They like cheese and beans and spuds.

If I had to swap the Spudwagons for another type of fast-food outlet, it would have to be pancakes. Really. I love pancakes. Or tacos. Birria tacos with a consommé. We need a birria beef baked potato with a consommé that we pour over the top in a wedge line. That'd be amazing.

My favourite chefs are the Hairy Bikers, all the way. Tom Kerridge is cool and he follows me on Instagram. Matt Tebbutt, who does *Saturday Morning Kitchen*, he's good. Obviously, Gordon Ramsay as well, because I like Ramsay. I've met his daughter Tilly, and she is lovely. I've watched the Sorted Food guys on YouTube pretty much since they started and I'm definitely a super fan!

But I've probably watched the Hairy Bikers more than I've watched anything. And I've cooked more of their recipes than I have anyone else's.

The best spud I've had from someone else is Mr Spud's, creamy mushroom chicken. Best baked potato I have had, hands down, anywhere. You can quote me on that. Fair enough.

Things don't always go to plan in the kitchen. I gave everyone food poisoning from ribs once. The family, that is. I had this really good idea and I got these ribs from the butchers, but they were really thick. I put them in for maybe three hours and they still were like underdone. Wasn't good.

Otherwise, it took me a long while to perfect the scotch egg, you know. It takes quite a lot of effort to get that runny inside. It took me a lot, a lot of tries, a lot of exploding scotch eggs.

And the future?

To be completely honest, I reckon I've got about ten years in me. Eight to ten years of doing this, and then I need to retire. I need to pay my mortgage off and then I need to build a monster truck.

Business-wise, I want to get Dylan set up. Eventually I kind of want him to take over from me in a sense; like I can do less, and he can do more. I want to help my kids grow in whatever business that they want to go into. So Honey-Willow wants to have a livery yard and I want to help her set that up.

Ultimately, I'd like to leave the world better fed and more community-spirited. Hopefully I can do that, in my own small way.

I'VE GOT NINE KIDS SO BAKED POTATOES ARE A STAPLE AT HOME. MY KIDS ARE BASIC THOUGH. THEY LIKE CHEESE AND BEANS AND SPUDS

SPUDHEALTH

Before my diagnosis, I was just a normal 20-year-old lad travelling to events with my spud trailer and doing festivals. That all changed when my kidneys failed, but through it all I've been determined to keep running my business, while accommodating my dialysis treatment.

My health problems began in 2010 when I failed a medical for life insurance and went to see my doctor. I did a blood test and was sent straight to hospital. That day I crash-landed into kidney failure and immediately started dialysis treatment. My kidney function was at just 8 per cent.

I was in complete denial. I thought doctors would fix me and get me on my way. Obviously, it didn't work out like that. I initially received peritoneal dialysis treatment but didn't get on well with it and moved to haemodialysis which was better.

Later on, I wanted to take back more control and moved to having my haemodialysis at home, but it was in 2015 while being treated in the dialysis unit that I met Sarah. Without my kidney failure we wouldn't have our life together.

Quite a few people with kidney problems come up to the trailer. I think they appreciate me showing a positive perspective on living with the illness and raising awareness.

I dialyse at home when I'm asleep because there's no time in the day. It's either work, kids or free time that I'm not going to give up. Thankfully I've been given the opportunity to have dialysis at home – I know not everyone has that. I've always worked for myself, which helps too because I can be flexible with my time off. If I was employed, I would've struggled more.

We try to show people that even though treatment is difficult, it's not the end of the world. It is inconvenient and the need to dialyse makes it harder to be away from home, but some people think without a transplant you'll just die.

I'm here to prove everyone wrong.

BECOMING SPUDWIFE

The woman I cared for back then had renal failure and we used to go into the unit during the afternoons for dialysis. As she was coming off her session, Ben would come in for his. We would ask after him because he was a bit of a unique patient. He used to paint his models and play on his Xbox, and we'd joke about him.

I then got a job on the unit because I felt the patient experience could have been better, and Ben ended up coming back in after his first transplant was unsuccessful. Now, here we are, nearly a decade later!

Ben has two boys from a previous relationship, and I've got my children, but we're lucky because we've had our four youngest babies while Ben has been on dialysis, which is quite rare. We're thankful for everything good in our lives. Dialysis is challenging but we don't let the kidney problems define us.

One of my proudest moments for Ben, was watching him walk back onto the dialysis unit knowing that he was never going to get another transplant, because I know how difficult that was for him.

It's a huge rollercoaster. Everyone thinks you're going to get this transplant and it'll just start working but that's not how it happens. You just go with it and make the best out of a rubbish situation. You can live a good life on dialysis, and there are a lot of people who do.

Ben is a very positive person but sometimes he finds it harder than he lets on. He'll bounce around the trailer and then come home feeling not so great. Dialysis affects the whole family, but we try our best to keep everything as normal as possible.

I plan my shifts around Ben's treatment, and we're lucky his dialysis equipment is portable enough to take with us in the car when we go away – even though it requires a lot of preparation.

Ben has a good relationship with his consultant which helps, and his dialysis team have always been so supportive. They genuinely care and organise get-togethers for patients to meet others with renal failure, so they feel less alone.

I'm proud of how much we've managed to do while on dialysis: having our children, running the business and going on holidays. We've had messages from people facing renal failure or starting dialysis, who are feeling down. They've told us that watching Ben helped them feel more positive that they can still live their life.

If you or anyone else you know is affected by kidney disease, help can be found at **kidneyresearchuk.org**

SPUD METHOD

Sometimes the simplest food is the hardest to get right, but I think I've perfected it. So I'm not reinventing the wheel here, and this will be familiar to anyone who bought the first book.

The secret to baked potatoes is to cook them hot and fast. The crispier the better. At home I do them unwrapped.

The cooking time depends on the size of the potato, but if it fits in your hand, you should probably cook it for about 1 hour 20 minutes at 220°C (fan 200°C).

Any larger, you're looking at more than 1 hour 30 minutes at least.

In the trailer we wrap them in foil and do them even hotter and even quicker. An industrial potato oven hits 300–350°C.

Don't always go for the largest potato you can find. A couple of smaller ones will cook more evenly and won't have any lumpy bits.

You don't need to prick them. That's a complete myth, and I've never seen a potato explode, like EV-ER.

Be patient and wait until they're ready. You can tell by giving the spud a little squeeze. If you feel like you could squeeze through it, it's ready. But it's got to have that give in it. We do it all by touch in the van, poking all of them. You need tough old hands.

What really makes baked potatoes the ultimate comfort food is butter. Lots of good quality butter, dripping out the side. Butter makes everything good, doesn't it?

Speed hack: microwave and then air fry your baked potato to ensure you still get a crispy skin. But only if you're short of time.

Do not ever reheat a baked potato. It's atrocious. Just eat it hot, and fast.

But really, it's not so much about how you cook the potato – it's the variety...

ALL OUR POTATOES COME FROM THE AMAZING GUYS AT LOWE'S POTATOES IN WARWICKSHIRE (HELLO DAVID, JANE, NIGEL AND HELEN!)

SPUD SUPPLIERS

All our potatoes come from the amazing guys at Lowe's Potatoes in Warwickshire (hello David, Jane, Nigel and Helen!), which is a third-generation family business founded in 1950. They supply all sorts of people from supermarkets, wholesalers, fam shops, local convenience stores, pubs and restaurants. There's every chance you've eaten one without knowing. And they're bloody delicious.

They're just really good growers. I think they've got good soil and the farm is on top of an aquifer, so they can just irrigate like crazy. They've always got good spuds, no matter the weather. We've bought off big companies before, but they turn over crops. They'll buy an entire farm's worth and go through it in a week, and then you're on to something else. So there's no consistency. Buying off a small farmer, you've got good consistency all year round. The price has dropped for potatoes this year but we carried on paying a fair price, even though we've been offered spuds elsewhere a for a lot cheaper. We want them to do well.

We use Marfona or Melody potatoes mainly. Marfonas are versatile all-rounders, fresh with a nice yellow skin and flesh and with a smooth, buttery taste packed full of flavour. I think they're from the Netherlands, originally. And Melodys have good taste and texture too, with smooth clean skins. Cara is a good variety, we used to use Estimas too. Growing up with a potato merchant for a dad, I know my potatoes!

I'd generally advise against buying Nadine potatoes, which are often stocked by supermarkets. They look good and crop well but the cook is often poor.

Booker

Booker's is my happy place, and the source of so much of what I do and make. Thank you to everyone who has helped me over the years, and especially to Kerry Drewett, Booker's development chef.

The Grate Cheese Company

Matt is my cheese man and has been for about twenty years. He's reliable, he rotates the stock and delivers early and on time. He's got me out of many a pickle, if you'll excuse the pun.

LOWE'S ARE JUST REALLY GOOD GROWERS. BUYING OFF A SMALL FARMER, YOU'VE GOT GOOD CONSISTENCY ALL YEAR ROUND

SPUDMATES

The humble baked potato has become a nationwide food sensation and I've been lucky enough to meet some really great people building businesses around the country. From the very first time I crossed paths with **John the Spud**, swapping tips on the best butter-to-topping ratio, to sharing pitches with **Mr Spud** and the unmistakable **Nae Just Spuds** up north — every one of them has shaped this daft, wonderful journey. **Smokey Mose**, **SpudMobile** and **Spud Fusion** have each brought their own flavour (literally) to the scene, and watching this whole spud movement grow has been one of the great joys of my life. What started as a few vans has become a proper phenomenon – and I'm proud to call so many of these guys family.

HERE'S A LITTLE RUN-DOWN OF SOME OF MY FAVES, IN TOP TRUMPS™ STYLE (THOUGH THEY'RE NOT REALLY COMPETING).

JOHN THE SPUD

Location: Liverpool

Years in the game: 28

Celebrity superfan: Paddy the Baddy

Number of ovens: 2

Signature topping: Chilli, cheese, crispy onion and honey chilli sauce

Best event: Christmas markets with… Spud Man

MR SPUD

Location: Stevenage

Years in the game: 2.5

Celebrity superfan: Sevda Ela

Number of ovens: 2

Signature topping: Creamy mushroom chicken

Best event: Oxford charity fireworks

NAE JUST SPUDS

Location: Aberdeen, Scotland

Years in the game: 1 and a bit!

Celebrity superfan: Graham Shinnie

Number of ovens: 3

Signature topping: Our Sunday dinner spuds

Best event: We're shop-based so our 12 Days of Christmas charity campaign

SMOKEY MOSE

Location: Dorset and the New Forest

Years in the game: 5

Celebrity superfan: Wonder Woman and Captain America

Number of ovens: 2 (up to 3)

Signature topping: Kickin' chicken

Best event: Wessex Events at Bryanston School

SPUDMOBILE

Location: Norwich

Years in the game: 1.5

Celebrity superfan: Does Spud Man count?

Number of ovens: 2

Signature topping: Royal roast dinner

Best event: Spud Man's visit, obvs!

SPUD FUSION

Location: Portsmouth

Years in the game: 1

Celebrity superman: Only Spud Man!

Number of ovens: 2

Signature topping: Mighty masala

Best event: Victorious

SPUD LIFE

This is more or less the lifespan of a British spud. Unless you forget to water them, or they get blight or some other disaster happens. Not me, though. Mine are always perfect.

CHITTING (JAN–FEB)

Seed potatoes should be set out in trays in a cool, light spot indoors to sprout short, sturdy shoots before planting. This gives them a head start against chilly soil.

PLANTING (MAR–APR)

First earlies go in from mid-March, second earlies and maincrop follow through April, once the soil has warmed enough and the worst frosts have passed.

HAULM GROWTH (APR–JUN)

Green leafy growth pushes up fast; you 'earth up' by mounding soil over the stems to stop developing tubers turning green in the light.

FLOWERING (JUN–JUL)

White, pink, or purple blossoms appear and that means tubers are forming underground.

HARVEST: EARLIES (JUN–AUG)

New potatoes are lifted just weeks after flowering, while the skins are still thin and delicate.

HARVEST: MAINCROP (SEP–OCT)

Left longer to bulk up, the main crop is dug once the leaves have died back, giving the classic baking and roasting spuds of autumn.

CURING & STORAGE (OCT–MAR)

Harvested potatoes are cured in a dark, cool, well-ventilated spot to toughen their skins, then stored through winter — potentially right up until next year's chitting begins, closing the loop.

GROWYEROWNSPUD

Keen to take that extra step towards Spud Man authenticity? No problem, grow your own! With Spud Man Seed Potatoes, you can cultivate the varieties I use to create my legendary spuds. Whether you're a seasoned grower or planting for the first time, Jamieson Brothers' premium-quality seed potatoes ensure high yields, and fantastic flavour.

These are certified seed potatoes, carefully chosen for strong disease resistance and consistent growth in UK soils. Whether you're planting in a raised bed, an allotment, or planter bags, you'll get healthy, productive plants with potatoes perfect for all types of culinary uses.

Backed by years of hands-on experience and a proper love of spuds, these seed potatoes are your first step to growing something seriously tasty.

There are many types of seed potatoes, and each one is grown for a different reason. Some are ready to harvest early, some take longer but produce bigger crops.

Here's a simple guide:

First early potatoes are the quickest to grow. They are planted in early spring and ready to harvest in about 10 to 12 weeks. They are smaller potatoes, perfect for boiling or using in salads.

Second early potatoes take a little longer. They are ready to harvest around 13 to 14 weeks after planting. They hold their shape well when cooked, making them great for salads and everyday meals.

Maincrop potatoes take the longest to grow but give you the biggest harvest. They are ready after about 16 to 20 weeks. These potatoes are ideal for roasting, baking, mashing, and making chips because of their bigger size and floury texture.

Buy the full range at Jamiesonbrothers.com

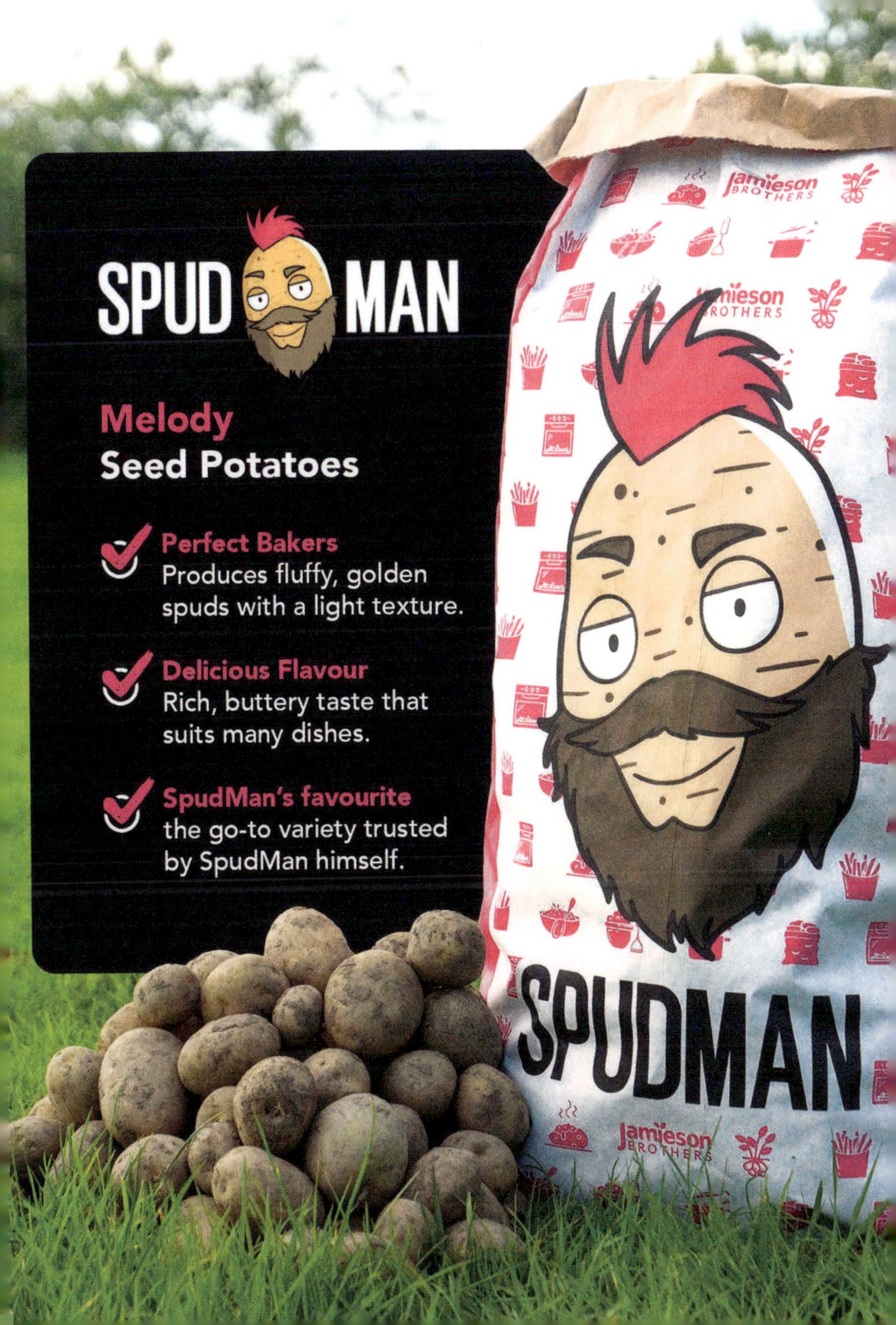
SPUD MAN
Melody
Seed Potatoes
Perfect Bakers
Produces fluffy, golden spuds with a light texture.
Delicious Flavour
Rich, buttery taste that suits many dishes.
SpudMan's favourite
the go-to variety trusted by SpudMan himself.
Jamieson BROTHERS
SPUDMAN
Jamieson BROTHERS

SPUDKIT

We have three wagons at the moment, plus all the stuff we need to keep them going like the prep gazebo, the van, the generators and all that gear.

We've still got the old wagon, the one we've kind of retired. We're keeping hold of it for Dylan and Lil Spud to get started up. So that's the little one – I'd say it's 18 feet. It got us to where we needed to be. It's not perfect; it was a cheap build. Then we've gone for the same size, but wider and better. That's our trailer for Tamworth. It's in a black livery with the pink and it looks beautiful. It's got the LEDs on it. Again, it was done to a bigger budget, but not a silly budget. Two ovens, two serving spots. You know, it's still very capable, but it's not the big boy. The big unit, the mega unit, my baby, has four ovens. Four serving spots. Hydraulic top signs. Hydraulic ovens. Starlink on the roof. It's the best spud unit in the world right now. No competition.

Our ovens are King Edwards and we had a big hand in designing these gas ovens. Four years ago, we went to James at King Edward and we said: Pickwicks, who used to make our ovens, don't exist anymore. We need some big gas ovens. King Edward only ever made electric ovens and we need a big gas oven. So, we decided to work together. Now we've got them to where we want them to be and they cook a beautiful potato. It's taken four prototypes to get to where we are, but it's working now.

I actually went in to collect my four new gas potato ovens from them in Bromyard last year. These ones even have my face on.

HOUSEKEEPING

When I say 'cheese', I usually mean our mix of cheese which is 80% Cheddar, 20% mozzarella. Unless I mention something else.

These recipes are intended for home cooking and small portions, therefore they'll be slightly different to the things you've seen me batch cook on the Spud Wagon. And some of those recipes are trade secrets so what you'll find here are recipes with a twist.

I'm told Americans don't call jacket spuds 'jacket spuds', so I only use the word 'baked' in this book. They're the same thing, though.

THERE'S NO SUCH THING AS TOO MUCH BUTTER!

KING
EDWARD
SPUD MAN

THE RECIPES

JANUARY

THE BBQ JACKFRUIT SPUD

It's January – a new year and a new you. Time to make some resolutions for the next 12 months. But if that seems like a very long time, how about signing up for Veganuary and giving up meat, fish, eggs and dairy for just a month? You can still enjoy your spuds and some very healthy fillings and tasty toppings, like this shredded jackfruit in BBQ sauce.

Serves 2 | Prep: 15 minutes | Cook: 10 minutes

2 x Spud Man baked potatoes

2 large knobs of plant-based butter

Spud Man Coleslaw (see page 41 and use plant-based mayo)

thinly sliced red onion

chopped coriander

salt and freshly ground black pepper

BBQ jackfruit topping

1 x 400g (14oz) tin of green jackfruit in brine, drained and rinsed

1 tsp light brown sugar

1 tsp smoked paprika

1 tsp chilli powder

½ tsp garlic powder

1 tbsp olive oil

120ml (4fl oz) smoky BBQ sauce

NEW YEAR... NEW SPUDS

1 Make the BBQ jackfruit: use your hands to gently squeeze out any water from the jackfruit, then pat dry with kitchen paper. Discard the seeds and core, and shred the jackfruit with two forks.

2 Transfer to a bowl and add the sugar, spices and garlic powder. Toss the jackfruit in the spice mixture until lightly coated.

3 Heat the oil in a frying pan set over a medium heat and cook the jackfruit, stirring occasionally, for 4–5 minutes, or until it starts to brown. Add 3 tablespoons cold water and continue cooking for 5 minutes, or until the liquid evaporates and the jackfruit is getting crisp. Stir in the BBQ sauce and remove from the heat.

4 Cut a large cross in the top of each Spud Man baked potato and gently squeeze the bottom to open up the top. Add a knob of butter and some salt and pepper. Place each one in a shallow bowl and top with the shredded BBQ jackfruit.

5 Add some coleslaw and sprinkle with the red onion and coriander, then dig in!

Smoky BBQ Sauce

You can use a ready-made BBQ sauce or make it yourself: place 300ml (½ pint) tomato ketchup, 3 tablespoons each light brown sugar and red wine vinegar, 2 tablespoons Worcestershire sauce (traditional Worcestershire sauce, such as Lea & Perrins, contains anchovy [fish] so ensure you use a vegan one e.g. Biona), 1 tablespoon each soy sauce and wholegrain or Dijon mustard, a squeeze of lemon juice and 2 teaspoons smoked paprika in a saucepan. Stir well and set over a medium heat. When it starts to bubble, cook for 5 minutes, then add to the crispy cooked jackfruit.

Tinned jackfruit is available in many supermarkets and health food shops as well as online.

10.00

THE BURNS NIGHT SPUD

A lovely baked spud (or tatties) filled with haggis and swede (neeps) and served in homemade onion gravy is the perfect way to celebrate Burns Night (25 January). And don't forget the wee dram of whisky to toast the haggis! You can buy ready-cooked meaty or plant-based haggis, which only needs reheating, in most supermarkets and online (always follow the instructions on the packet).

Serves 2 | Prep: 15 minutes | Cook: 20–30 minutes

2 x Spud Man baked potatoes

2 large knobs of butter

salt and freshly ground black pepper

Haggis and neeps topping

300g (10oz) swede, peeled and cubed

30g (1oz) butter

2 tbsp milk

400g (14oz) haggis (traditional meat or vegetarian)

Onion gravy

2 tbsp olive oil

1 onion, thinly sliced

1 tbsp plain flour

150ml (5fl oz) beef, chicken or vegetable stock

1–2 tbsp balsamic vinegar

a dash of Worcestershire sauce

The quickest way to reheat the haggis is in a microwave. It's ready in less than 5 minutes!

1 Place the swede in a pan of salted water and bring to the boil. Cook for 15 minutes, or until it is tender and cooked right through. Drain well and return to the pan. Mash with the butter and milk and season to taste with salt and pepper.

2 Meanwhile, reheat the haggis according to the instructions on the packet (in the oven, on the hob or in the microwave) while you make the gravy.

3 Make the onion gravy: heat the oil in a frying pan set over a low heat. Add the onion and cook for 15 minutes, stirring occasionally, until tender and starting to caramelize. Stir in the flour and cook for 1 minute. Add the stock, vinegar and Worcestershire sauce and bring to the boil, stirring. Reduce the heat and let it bubble gently for 4–5 minutes until thickened and smooth. Season to taste.

4 Cut a large cross in the top of each Spud Man baked potato and gently squeeze the bottom to open up the top. Add a knob of butter and some salt and pepper. Transfer to two serving bowls and top with the haggis and swede. Pour the gravy over the top and serve piping hot!

THE RESOLUTION-BREAKER

These eggs-and-bacon-loaded spuds with a dash of spicy mango chutney or chilli sauce make a tasty and satisfying breakfast or brunch on the morning after your Dry January ambitions have been thwarted! Don't worry ... it happens, and at least you get to enjoy these lovely spuds.

Serves 2 | Prep: 15 minutes | Cook: 15 minutes

2 x large Spud Man baked potatoes

2 large knobs of butter
2–3 tbsp milk
60g (2oz) grated Cheddar cheese
4 small eggs
4 back bacon rashers
a few chives, chopped
spicy mango chutney or Sriracha
salt and freshly ground black pepper

Make sure you use large baking potatoes to create enough room for the eggs.

1 Preheat the oven to 190°C (170°C fan/375°F).

2 Cut the cooked Spud Man baked potatoes in half and spoon out the flesh, leaving about 5mm (¼ inch) potato inside each skin to form a shell.

3 Mash the potato flesh in a bowl with the butter and milk until smooth and season with salt and pepper, to taste. Stir in the Cheddar and spoon the mixture into the potato shells. Using a spoon, make a hollow in the centre of each one and crack in an egg.

4 Transfer to a baking tray and bake in the oven for 15 minutes, or until the egg whites are set and the yolks are still a little runny.

5 While the eggs are cooking, fry or grill the bacon until crispy and golden, then drain on kitchen paper.

6 Serve the potatoes straight from the oven and crumble the bacon over the top. Sprinkle with chives and add a big spoonful of spicy mango chutney or a good drizzle of Sriracha.

THE DETOX DELIGHT

A great restorative spud for when you're recovering from all the Christmas and New Year excess and too much rich food. It's time to get back to basics with some healthy green veggies, herbs, gut-friendly yoghurt and goat's cheese. You'll thank me for this.

Serves 2 | Prep: 15 minutes | Cook: 6–8 minutes

2 x Spud Man baked potatoes

2 large knobs of butter

2–3 tbsp milk

4 thick slices of goat's cheese log (chèvre)

warm honey

salt and freshly ground black pepper

Detox filling

¼ Savoy or green cabbage, heart cut out and thinly sliced

1 large leek, trimmed and thinly sliced

a few chives, chopped, plus extra for the top

2–3 tbsp natural yoghurt

You can use seasonal spring greens or fresh or frozen spinach instead of cabbage.

1 Make the detox filling: bring a pan of salted water to the boil and add the cabbage and leek. When the water comes back to the boil, reduce the heat and simmer for 4–5 minutes, or until just tender. Drain well.

2 Cut the cooked Spud Man baked potatoes in half and spoon out the flesh, leaving about 5mm (¼ inch) potato inside each skin to form a shell.

3 Mash the potato flesh in a bowl with the butter and milk until smooth and season with salt and pepper, to taste. Stir in the cabbage and leek along with the chives and yoghurt.

4 Spoon the mixture into the potato shells and top each one with a slice of goat's cheese. Pop under a preheated hot grill for 1–2 minutes until the cheese is bubbling and golden. Serve immediately, drizzled with some warm honey and garnished with a few chopped chives.

DON'T GO EASY ON IT
Garlic Butter

FEBRUARY

LOVE IS IN THE AIR

THE CORNED BEEF JACK ONE

This winter warmer is a golden oldie from cold evenings spent at my nan's house. I love corned beef – it's nostalgia in every bite. Brings back so many happy memories. You don't have to add a dollop of coleslaw. We used to devour plain baked spuds slathered with butter with mashed-up corned beef, some grated Cheddar and lots of brown sauce. Lovely!

Serves 2 | Prep: 15 minutes

2 x Spud Man baked potatoes

2 large knobs of butter

6 slices of corned beef

85g (3oz) grated Cheddar cheese or mixed Cheddar and mozzarella (see page 26)

2 large spoonfuls of crispy fried onions

a good dash of brown sauce or Worcestershire sauce

salt and freshly ground black pepper

Spud Man's world-famous coleslaw

2 large carrots, grated

½ red cabbage, heart cut out and shredded

1 large red onion, shredded

4–6 heaped tbsp mayo

1 Make the coleslaw: place all the prepared vegetables in a large bowl and mix in enough mayo to bind everything together. You want it nice and creamy. Season with salt and pepper.

2 Cut a large cross in the top of each Spud Man baked potato and gently squeeze the bottom to open up the top. Add a knob of butter and some salt and pepper. Transfer to two serving bowls and top with the corned beef. Chop it up into the potato and then sprinkle with cheese and crispy onions. Add a dash of sauce and lots of coleslaw.

Don't add salt to the coleslaw as it draws out the moisture in your vegetables – you don't want sloppy coleslaw!

MARRY ME CHICKEN (OR QUORN) SPUD

This is heaven on a potato – it's tomatoey, rich and lush – an absolute winner for Valentine's Day. And if you make my creamy meat-free veggie version with Quorn (go to the end of the recipe), you'll be amazed – you won't believe it's not chicken.

Serves 2 | Prep: 10 minutes | Cook: 20–25 minutes

2 x Spud Man baked potatoes

2 large knobs of butter

a few basil leaves

salt and freshly ground black pepper

Marry Me chicken topping

2 tbsp plain flour

2 chicken breasts, skinless and cut into chunks

2 tbsp olive oil

1 onion, finely chopped

60g (2oz) sun-dried tomatoes in oil, chopped, plus 1 tbsp oil for frying

2 garlic cloves, crushed

6 cherry tomatoes on-the-vine

1 tbsp tomato paste

200g (7oz) tinned chopped tomatoes

a pinch each of dried thyme and oregano

1 tsp sweet paprika

½–1 tsp chilli flakes

120ml (4fl oz) chicken stock

100ml (3½fl oz) double cream

45g (1½oz) grated Parmesan or mixed Cheddar and mozzarella (see page 26)

1 Place the flour and some salt and pepper in a sealable plastic bag and add the chicken chunks. Shake well until the chicken is coated all over. Shake off any excess.

2 Heat the oil in a large frying pan set over a medium heat. Add the chicken and fry for 6–8 minutes or until browned and cooked right through. Remove from the pan and drain on kitchen paper. Set aside.

3 Add the onion to the pan with oil from the jar of sun-dried tomatoes and cook for 4–5 minutes. Add the garlic, sun-dried tomatoes, whole cherry tomatoes and tomato paste. Stir well and cook gently for a few minutes before adding the tinned chopped tomatoes, herbs, paprika and chilli flakes.

CONTINUED OVERLEAF...

4 Pour in the stock and cook for 5 minutes or until the sauce starts to thicken. Lower the heat to a simmer and stir in the cream and Parmesan. Cook gently for 2–3 minutes. You can leave the sauce chunky or use a stick blender to break down the big bits. It needs to be quite smooth – not like baby food. Stir in the chicken and simmer for a few more minutes.

5 Cut a large cross in the top of each Spud Man baked potato and gently squeeze the bottom to open up the top. Add a knob of butter and some salt and pepper. Transfer to two serving bowls and top with the Marry Me chicken and sauce. Scatter with basil leaves and enjoy!

Marry Me Quorn

Ignore steps 1 and 2 above and start at step 3 with frying the onion. Follow the recipe, substituting vegetable stock for the chicken stock and grated Cheddar for the Parmesan (unless using veggie Parmesan). After blending the sauce, stir in 300g (10oz) Quorn pieces and simmer for 8–10 minutes before serving with the baked spuds. Spudelicious!

IF SPUDWIFE HADN'T ALREADY MARRIED ME, SHE WOULD DO AFTER TASTING THIS

SPUDS OF FRIENDSHIP

A cosy night in is always a good idea when it's wet or cold at this time of year. So why not invite some friends round for a fun platter of Spud Man's loaded potato skins with some delicious toppings? You'll love these!

Serves 4–6 | Prep: 20 minutes | Cook: 25 minutes

8 x Spud Man baked potatoes

mustard

tomato ketchup

Sriracha

sour cream

salt and freshly ground black pepper

Vegan black beans topping

a glug of olive oil

1 small red onion, diced

1 red pepper, deseeded and diced

1 yellow pepper, deseeded and diced

2 garlic cloves, crushed

1 red chilli, shredded

6 cherry tomatoes, diced

200g (7oz) tinned black beans, drained

2–3 tbsp plant-based yoghurt, e.g. soya or coconut, plus extra for the top

60g (2oz) grated vegan cheese, e.g. mozzarella

Melty French cheese topping

1 tbsp olive oil

60g (2oz) unsalted butter

2 large onions, thinly sliced

a few sprigs of parsley, chopped

200g (7oz) ripe Camembert, rind removed and diced

Cheese and crispy bacon topping

100g (3½oz) streaky bacon, chopped

100g (3½oz) grated Cheddar cheese

Don't throw away the scooped-out potato – mash it with some milk and butter and reheat it for tomorrow's supper.

NORMALLY I WOULDN'T SHARE A SPUD, BUT FOR THESE I'LL MAKE AN EXCEPTION

1 Preheat the oven to 200°C (180°C fan/400°F).

2 Cut the cooked Spud Man baked potatoes in half and spoon out the flesh, leaving about 5mm (¼ inch) potato inside each skin to form a shell. Season lightly with salt and pepper.

3 Vegan black beans topping: heat the oil in a frying pan set over a medium heat and cook the onion, peppers, garlic and chilli for 6–8 minutes until softened. Add the tomatoes and beans and cook for 3–4 minutes. Season to taste and stir in the yoghurt. Spoon the mixture into four or five potato shells and sprinkle the cheese over the top. Cook in the oven for 6–8 minutes until golden brown and the cheese melts.

4 Melty French cheese topping: heat the oil and two-thirds of the butter in a frying pan set over a low heat. When the butter melts, add the onion and cook gently for 12–15 minutes, until tender and golden brown. Transfer to a bowl and mix with the parsley and Camembert. Season with salt and pepper and spoon into four or five potato shells. Place on a baking tray and top with the remaining butter. Cook in the oven for 10 minutes until golden brown.

5 Cheese and crispy bacon topping: cook the bacon in a frying pan set over a medium to high heat for 3 minutes until golden brown and crispy. Fill the remaining potato shells with the bacon and cheese and cook in the oven for 6–8 minutes until golden brown and bubbling.

6 Arrange the loaded skins on a large serving plate and dig in. Serve with mustard, ketchup, Sriracha, sour cream and more yoghurt.

MARDI GRAS MADNESS

In New Orleans, February is carnival time and the final day, Mardi Gras, always falls on the day before the beginning of Lent. Traditionally, everyone tucks into meat and fish and rich, fatty foods before the fasting begins. So, try my Creole-style spuds oozing with seafood, cream, melted cheese and spicy flavours. They're a great way to treat yourself and escape those February blues. And yes, there's a lot of prawns and crab... they're LOADED!

Serves 2 | Prep: 15 minutes | Cook: 25–30 minutes

2 x Spud Man baked potatoes

2 large knobs of butter

225g (8oz) grated cheese, e.g. Cheddar, Parmesan or Gruyère

salt and freshly ground black pepper

Creole-style seafood filling

1 tsp Cajun seasoning

1 tsp onion powder

½ tsp chilli flakes

1 tsp paprika

225g (8oz) raw king prawns, shelled and deveined

225g (8oz) white crab meat (fresh or frozen and defrosted or tinned)

2 tsp olive oil

2 tbsp unsalted butter

1 small onion, finely chopped

1 small red pepper, deseeded and diced

2 garlic cloves, crushed

150ml (5fl oz) double cream

1 Preheat the oven to 200°C (180°C fan/400°F).

2 Cut the cooked Spud Man baked potatoes in half and spoon out the flesh, leaving about 5mm (¼ inch) potato inside each skin to form a shell. Place the shells on a baking tray.

3 Mash the scooped-out potato with the butter. Season lightly with salt and pepper. Cover and set aside.

4 Mix the Cajun seasoning with the onion powder, chilli flakes and paprika in a bowl. Add the prawns and crab meat and stir gently until lightly coated.

5 Heat the oil and butter in a frying pan set over a medium heat and cook the seafood for 1–2 minutes until the prawns are pink underneath. Turn the seafood over and cook the other side. Remove.

6 Add the onion, red pepper and garlic to the pan and cook for 5 minutes or until the vegetables soften. Stir in the cream and simmer for 2–3 minutes until heated through.

7 Spoon half of the potato filling into the shells and top with a layer of cheese and some of the creamy sauce. Add a layer of seafood, some more cheese and then some more potato. Keep layering up in this way, finishing with a layer of cheese.

8 Bake in the oven for 15 minutes, or until the cheese has melted and the potatoes are appetizingly golden brown.

TREAT YOURSELF AND ESCAPE THOSE FEBRUARY BLUES

MARCH

SPRING INTO SPUDS

A CAWL CYMREIG SPUD

Simple and tasty, cawl Cymreig (Welsh soup) is a traditional dish eaten in Wales on St David's Day (1 March). Packed with root vegetables, leeks and lamb, it's the perfect topping for your baked spuds on the first day of spring. If you don't like lamb, don't worry – you can make it with beef (skirt or stewing beef) or even ham hock instead.

Serves 2 | Prep: 15 minutes | Cook: 1 hour

2 x Spud Man baked potatoes

2 large knobs of butter

2 handfuls of grated Caerphilly cheese

salt and freshly ground black pepper

Cawl Cymreig topping

350g (12oz) stewing lamb, e.g. neck, cut into chunks

1 onion, chopped

2 small leeks, trimmed and sliced

1 large carrot, sliced

225g (8oz) swede, peeled and cubed

a handful of parsley, chopped

For a really tasty cawl, you can make it the day before and chill in a sealed container in the fridge overnight or for 2–3 days. When you're ready to eat it with your spuds, just reheat gently in a pan on the hob.

1 Place the lamb in a saucepan with 500ml (17fl oz) cold water and ½ teaspoon salt. Set over a high heat and bring to the boil, using a slotted spoon to skim off any scum that rises to the surface. Reduce the heat and simmer gently for 15–20 minutes.

2 Add the onion, leek, carrot and swede and bring back to the boil. Reduce the heat and simmer for 30 minutes, or until the lamb is tender and the vegetables are cooked. Stir in the parsley and season to taste with salt and pepper.

3 Cut a large cross in the top of each Spud Man baked potato and gently squeeze the bottom to open up the top. Add a knob of butter and some salt and pepper. Transfer to two serving bowls and ladle the cawl over the top. Sprinkle with a handful of Caerphilly and enjoy. The potato will soak up some of the delicious stock.

Cawl is more soupy than most stews, so you can reduce the stock before serving, if you like.

INSTEAD OF SMASHING UP AN AVOCADO FOR THE FILLING, STIR SOME TINNED CHICKPEAS OR BEANS INTO A BOUGHT CREAMY GREEN GODDESS DRESSING AND DRIZZLE WITH THE PESTO

THE GREEN GODDESS

Spring has sprung and it's time for some spudtastic new ways to enjoy my baked potatoes. Let's start with my Green Goddess spud, oozing with melted garlic butter and topped with a fresh pea and herb pesto and smashed avocado. If you like the hot stuff, drizzle it with some sweet chilli sauce or Sriracha. Yum yum.

Serves 2 | Prep: 10–15 minutes | Cook: 5–6 minutes

2 x Spud Man baked potatoes

60g (2oz) unsalted butter

4 garlic cloves, crushed

1 large avocado, peeled and stone removed

a pinch of chilli flakes (optional)

Sriracha or sweet chilli sauce (optional)

grated Parmesan or Swiss cheese (optional)

salt and freshly ground black pepper

Pea and herb pesto

85g (3oz) podded fresh peas (or frozen and thawed)

1 tbsp pine nuts

1–2 garlic cloves

a handful of fresh mint (or basil if you prefer)

3 tbsp grated Parmesan

1–2 tbsp olive oil

a squeeze of lemon juice

1 Make the pea and herb pesto: if you're using fresh peas, cook them in a pan of boiling water for 3 minutes, until tender. Drain in a colander and plunge into a bowl of cold water. Drain and pat dry with kitchen paper.

2 Toast the pine nuts in a dry frying pan until lightly browned.

3 Pulse the peas, garlic cloves, herbs, pine nuts, cheese, olive oil and lemon juice in a blender or food processor until blended and slightly grainy – not too smooth. Check the seasoning and add more cheese, herbs or lemon juice if you think they're needed.

4 Cut a large cross in the top of each Spud Man baked potato and gently squeeze the bottom to open up the top. Melt the butter with the crushed garlic in a pan set over a low to medium heat, then pour into the potatoes. Season with salt and pepper.

5 Smash the avocado flesh with a fork – not too smooth, it should be a bit lumpy. Mash in the chilli flakes, if using, season and spoon into and over the potatoes. Drizzle with the pesto and serve if you like with some chilli sauce and grated cheese.

THE SPICE BAG SPECIAL

To celebrate St Patrick's Day, cook my Spice Bag spud. It's easy to make, quick to cook and will get you into the party mood. You'll be on fire after all those chillies! Add the finishing touch with a drizzle (or drenching) of (shop-bought) chip shop curry sauce.

Serves 2 | Prep: 15 minutes | Cook: 6–7 minutes

2 x Spud Man baked potatoes

60g (2oz) unsalted butter

Curry sauce, shop-bought

salt and freshly ground black pepper

Salt and chilli crispy chicken

250g (9oz) skinless boneless chicken thighs, cut into bite-sized cubes

1 egg, beaten

1 tbsp vegetable oil, plus extra for frying

½ green or red pepper, deseeded and thinly sliced

2 garlic cloves, crushed

3 spring onions, thinly sliced

1 red bird's eye chilli, diced

½ tsp chilli flakes

Spice bag

½ tsp salt

½ tsp freshly ground black pepper

¼ tsp garlic powder

¼ tsp Chinese 5 spice powder

¼ tsp smoked paprika

115g (4oz) cornflour

1 Dip the chicken into the beaten egg.

2 Place all the ingredients for the spice bag in a sealable plastic bag and shake gently until well mixed. Transfer to a bowl and use to coat the chicken.

3 Pour enough vegetable oil to cover the chicken into a large wok or deep frying pan. Set over a medium to high heat and when it reaches 180°C (350°F) (use a sugar thermometer to check) add the coated chicken and fry for 3–4 minutes until cooked right through, golden brown and crispy. Remove and drain on kitchen paper.

4 Heat 1 tablespoon of oil in a clean frying pan and set over a medium heat. Stir-fry the green or red pepper, garlic, spring onions and fresh chilli for 2 minutes, or until just tender. Stir in the chilli flakes and the chicken and toss gently.

5 Cut a large cross in the top of each Spud Man baked potato and gently squeeze the bottom to open up the top. Add a knob of butter and some salt and pepper. Transfer to two serving bowls and divide the salt and chilli crispy chicken mixture between them. Drizzle with plenty of curry sauce and tuck in while it's piping hot.

APRIL

THE SUNDAY ROAST SPUD

The perfect spud for St George's Day and Shakespeare Day, which both fall on 23 April. You can roast a small piece of beef separately for the occasion or just use leftovers from the Sunday roast. I like to keep it simple with peas and carrots, but you can swap them for any veggies – fresh or reheated leftovers. The golden parsnip crisps add a sweet and crispy flourish that you're going to thank me for. I guarantee you'll be making them again.

Serves 2 | Prep: 15 minutes | Cook: 20–25 minutes

2 x Spud Man baked potatoes

2 large knobs of butter

mustard or horseradish sauce

salt and freshly ground black pepper

Sunday roast topping

4–6 baby carrots, scrubbed or peeled

115g (4oz) peas (podded fresh or frozen)

4–6 slices of roast beef, warmed

Onion Gravy (see page 33)

Parsnip crisps

300g (10oz) parsnips, peeled

1 tbsp olive oil

a good pinch of smoked paprika

sea salt flakes

EASTER DELIGHTS

1 Make the parsnip crisps: preheat the oven to 180°C (160°C fan/350°F). If the parsnips are round and fat, use a mandolin or peeler to cut them into really thin rounds. If they are long and thin, peel long strips off them. Use kitchen paper to pat them dry.

2 Transfer them to a bowl and toss with the olive oil and smoked paprika. Spread them out in a single layer on two baking trays and bake for 20–25 minutes, turning them halfway through, until they are golden and starting to crisp around the edges. Sprinkle with sea salt flakes and set aside to cool.

3 While the parsnip crisps are baking, cook the carrots and peas in a pan of boiling water until tender. Drain well.

4 Cut a large cross in the top of each Spud Man baked potato and gently squeeze the bottom to open up the top. Add a knob of butter and some salt and pepper. Transfer to two serving bowls and add the roast beef and cooked vegetables. Pour some gravy over the top and around the spuds, then top with some parsnip crisps. Serve immediately with mustard or horseradish.

You can make the parsnip crisps in advance, but they are best eaten on the day they are made. Use up any leftover crisps with a pre-lunch or dinner drink.

THE EGG-CELLENT SPUD

Nothing beats a baked spud topped with creamy scrambled eggs and fiery chorizo for breakfast, brunch, supper or, indeed, at any time of the day. It's an easy meal when you're feeling peckish over the Easter holiday weekend – quick, too, if you cook some potatoes in advance and reheat them (though fresh is always better).

Serves 2 | Prep: 10 minutes | Cook: 8–12 minutes

2 x Spud Man baked potatoes

2 large knobs of butter

60g (2oz) grated Cheddar cheese

85g (3oz) chorizo, diced

salt and freshly ground black pepper

Scrambled egg topping

4 large eggs

a few chives, chopped

1 knob of butter

1 Cut a large cross in the top of each Spud Man baked potato and gently squeeze the bottom to open up the top. Add a knob of butter and some salt and pepper and mash in the cheese with a fork.

2 Set a frying pan over a medium to high heat and when it's hot, add the chorizo. Cook, stirring often, for 5–7 minutes, or until the chorizo is browned and crispy and all its red oil has been released. Remove with a slotted spoon and drain on kitchen paper.

3 Make the scrambled eggs: crack the eggs into a bowl, add a little salt and pepper and the chives and lightly beat them.

4 Melt the butter in a small saucepan set over a medium heat. Pour in the beaten egg and cook, stirring constantly with a wooden spoon, until the eggs start to scramble (about 3–5 minutes). Take the pan off the heat and continue stirring until they are creamy and set. Do not overcook them.

5 Pile on top of the baked potatoes. Sprinkle with the chorizo and get stuck in!

If you're not looking for heat and spice, substitute fried diced bacon or pancetta for the chorizo.

THE LAMB TAGINE

If you're bored with roast lamb and mint sauce every Easter, make my spicy lamb tagine instead. Slow cooking helps to tenderize the meat and enhance all the lovely spicy, fruity flavours. I reduce mine until it is thick and richly spiced – perfect for topping your Easter spuds. You can use a slow cooker, but the sauce may not reduce so much and won't be as thick.

Serves 2 | Prep: 10 minutes | Cook: 1¾–2 hours

2 x Spud Man baked potatoes

2 large knobs of butter

toasted almonds

chopped coriander

pomegranate seeds

salt and freshly ground black pepper

Lamb tagine topping

300g (10oz) lean lamb shoulder (fat removed), cut into chunks

2 tbsp olive or vegetable oil

1 onion, finely chopped

1 carrot, cut into chunks

3 garlic cloves, crushed

2 tbsp ras-el-hanout

1 tbsp tomato paste

2.5cm (1 inch) piece of fresh ginger, peeled and grated

350ml (12fl oz) chicken or veg stock

1 cinnamon stick

85g (3oz) whole dried apricots

Lamb shoulder is the best cut for slow cooking and it will be intensely flavoured and meltingly tender. If it's not available, use boneless lamb shank or leg, but these are leaner.

SLOW COOKING HELPS TO TENDERIZE THE MEAT AND ENHANCE ALL THE LOVELY SPICY, FRUITY FLAVOURS

1 Preheat the oven to 180°C (160°C fan/350°F).

2 Season the lamb with some salt and pepper. Heat the oil in a flameproof casserole dish set over a medium to high heat and cook the lamb, in batches, for 3–4 minutes, stirring occasionally, until it's browned all over. Remove and set aside.

3 Reduce the heat to medium and cook the onion and carrot for 5–6 minutes, until softened. Add the garlic and cook for 1 minute, then stir in the ras-el-hanout. Cook for 1 minute and add the tomato paste and ginger. Cook for 2–3 minutes, stirring, then add the lamb.

4 Add the stock and cinnamon stick and give it a stir, then cover the pan with a lid and cook for 1 hour. Stir in the apricots and if the sauce has reduced too much and there's not enough liquid, just add a little water. Return to the oven for 30–45 minutes until the sauce is thick and the lamb is falling apart.

5 Cut a large cross in the top of each Spud Man baked potato and gently squeeze the bottom to open up the top. Add a knob of butter and some salt and pepper. Place in two serving bowls and spoon the lamb tagine over the top. Sprinkle with toasted almonds, coriander and pomegranate seeds. Enjoy!

I'VE DONE A LOT OF TOURING THIS SUMMER:

BURTON UPON TRENT
BIGGLESWADE
STOKE MANDEVILLE
WREXHAM
CLEETHORPES
AND DERBY

BAKED POTATO

MAY

MAY DAY MAGIC

THE GARDEN PARTY SPUD

Most of us love May, not just because it's warmer and feels more summery, but also because we get TWO long weekends: May Day and Spring bank holiday. So, get out into the garden and treat yourself to my lovely baked spuds topped with salmon and spring veggies. Time to party!

Serves 2 | Prep: 15 minutes | Cook: 15 minutes

2 x Spud Man baked potatoes

2 large knobs of butter

salt and freshly ground black pepper

Garden party topping

2 x 115g (4oz) salmon fillets

olive oil or melted butter

4 lemon slices, plus grated zest of ½ lemon

115g (4oz) asparagus, cut into 2.5cm (1 inch) lengths

150g (5oz) spring greens or spinach

120ml (4fl oz) crème fraîche

chopped chives, mint or tarragon

1 Make the garden party topping: preheat the oven to 190°C (170°C fan/375°F). Place the salmon on a sheet of foil or baking parchment. Brush with oil or melted butter and place the lemon slices on top. Season with salt and pepper, then loosely fold the foil or baking parchment over the salmon to enclose it and seal the edges. Bake in the oven for 15 minutes, or until the salmon is cooked through and flakes easily.

2 Meanwhile, steam the asparagus tips in a steamer basket or colander over a saucepan of boiling water for 4–5 minutes, or until tender. Remove and set aside. Add the spring greens or spinach to the steamer or colander and cook for 2 minutes, until wilted.

3 Mix the crème fraîche with the chopped herbs and lemon zest.

4 Cut a large cross in the top of each Spud Man baked potato and gently squeeze the bottom to open up the top. Add a knob of butter and some salt and pepper. Fill with the herby crème fraîche and place a salmon fillet on top. Scatter the steamed greens on and around the potatoes.

To spice this up, sprinkle a few chilli flakes over the salmon and greens, add a dash of harissa or drizzle with some fiery hot sauce!

You don't have to use mayo – why not toss the slaw in a wasabi dressing instead? Place 1 tablespoon each light soy sauce, rice vinegar, caster sugar and sesame oil in a screwtop jar. Add 1 crushed garlic clove and 1 teaspoon wasabi paste and shake well.

THE SWICY SLAW SPUD

Sweet and spicy... this is my amazing swicy slaw spud with Japanese umami flavours. Sounds exotic? Well, basically it's just a variation on my classic Spud Man coleslaw and well worth making. If you're into Asian flavours and want to go all the way, you could top with some sashimi (thinly sliced very fresh raw fish) and a drizzle of soy sauce.

Serves 2 | Prep: 20 minutes

2 x Spud Man baked potatoes

2 large knobs of butter

thinly sliced smoked salmon (optional)

chopped coriander

sweet chilli sauce

salt and freshly ground black pepper

Swicy Spud Man slaw

¼ small red or white cabbage, heart cut out and shredded

1 large carrot, thinly sliced

2 spring onions, shredded

6 radishes, shredded

1 small red apple, cored and thinly sliced (or grated)

juice of ½ lemon

1 red chilli, shredded

4 tbsp mayo

1–2 tsp wasabi paste

a few drops of soy sauce

1 Make the swicy slaw: place all the prepared vegetables in a bowl. Squeeze a little lemon juice over the apple and stir into the vegetables with the chilli.

2 In a small bowl, mix together the mayo with the wasabi paste, adding it 1 teaspoon at a time, so the heat is to your liking. And then add 1–2 drops of soy sauce for flavour.

3 Gently stir the wasabi mayo into the slaw until everything is lightly coated.

4 Cut a large cross in the top of each Spud Man baked potato and gently squeeze the bottom to open up the top. Add a knob of butter and some salt and pepper, plus the salmon, if using. Divide the slaw between the potatoes and sprinkle with coriander before drizzling with sweet chilli sauce.

TASTY TUNA NIÇOISE

It's May and warmer weather has arrived – just in time for my baked potatoes with Spud Man's special tuna niçoise salad topping. Sooooo good!

Serves 2 | Prep: 15 minutes | Cook: 8 minutes

2 x Spud Man baked potatoes

2 large knobs of butter

salt and freshly ground black pepper

Tuna niçoise topping

115g (4oz) fine green beans, trimmed

2 eggs

1 x 145g (5oz) tin of tuna in spring water, drained

3 tbsp mayo

4 spring onions, thinly sliced

6 black olives, stones removed and sliced

2 tsp capers

2 sun-dried tomatoes, chopped

100g (3½oz) cherry tomatoes, quartered

a dash of lemon juice

a few sprigs of parsley, chopped

Instead of mayo, you could toss everything in a lemony, mustardy vinaigrette dressing.

1 Cook the green beans in a pan of boiling water for 4 minutes, or until just tender but still firm. Drain and rinse under cold running water.

2 Meanwhile, boil the eggs for 8 minutes. Place in a bowl of cold water and set aside. When they're cold, peel and cut into quarters or slices.

3 Mash the tuna lightly with a fork and mix with the mayo in a bowl. Add half of the spring onions, olives, capers and tomatoes, then fold in gently. Season to taste with salt and pepper and a dash of lemon juice.

4 Cut a large cross in the top of each Spud Man baked potato and gently squeeze the bottom to open up the top. Add a knob of butter and some salt and pepper.

5 Place in two serving bowls and fill with the tuna mayo mixture. Top with the eggs, green beans and the remaining spring onion, olives, capers and tomatoes. Sprinkle with the parsley and serve.

JUNE

SUMMER SIZZLERS

MEDITERRANEAN MAGIC

To get you in the mood for summer holidays and sunshine, make my baked spuds topped with roasted Mediterranean veggies: peppers, courgette and red onion with grilled halloumi. If it's a nice day, you could even get the barbie out, fire up the charcoal and cook them on the grill.

Serves 2 | Prep: 15 minutes | Cook: 25–30 minutes

2 x Spud Man baked potatoes

125g (4½oz) halloumi, cut into slices

2 large knobs of butter

2 tbsp green pesto

a few basil leaves

salt and freshly ground black pepper

Roasted veggie topping

2 red or yellow peppers, deseeded and cut into chunks

1 large courgette, cut into chunks

1 red onion, cut into wedges

4 garlic cloves in their skins

olive oil

Roast the vegetables while the baked spuds are cooking, or thread together with the halloumi on some kebab skewers, brushing them lightly with olive oil and cooking under a hot grill or on the BBQ for 10–15 minutes for a slightly smoky flavour.

1 Preheat the oven to 200°C (180°C fan/400°F). Place the vegetables in a roasting pan and tuck in the garlic cloves. Drizzle with olive oil until everything is coated. Roast in the oven for 25–30 minutes, or until the vegetables are tender. Squeeze the garlic out of their skins and mix into the vegetables.

2 Meanwhile, set a ridged grill pan over a medium heat and when it's hot, add the halloumi. Dry-fry for 2–3 minutes each side, until crisp and golden brown with slightly charred stripes. Remove, drain on kitchen paper and cut into smaller pieces.

3 Cut a large cross in the top of each Spud Man baked potato and gently squeeze the bottom to open up the top. Add a knob of butter and some salt and pepper. Place the potatoes in two bowls and top with the roasted vegetables and halloumi. Drizzle with the pesto and scatter with some fresh basil leaves. Breathe in deeply, take a big bite and savour the aroma and taste of summer.

PARTY-TIME PIZZA SPUD

My pizza spuds are seriously good and tasty – real comfort food. They're easy to make and perfect for parties and family get-togethers. Oozing with creamy mozzarella and loaded with spicy pepperoni and veggies... What's not to like?

Serves 6 | Prep: 10 minutes | Cook: 12–15 minutes

6 x Spud Man baked potatoes

6 large knobs of butter

green salad

salt and freshly ground black pepper

Pizza topping

180ml (6fl oz) tomato or pizza sauce (tinned, bottled or homemade)

60g (2oz) sliced pepperoni

12 mushrooms, sliced (or sliced chargrilled or roasted peppers)

1 ball of mozzarella, drained

green or red pesto

To make loaded potatoes, cut the baked potatoes in half and scoop out the flesh, leaving about 5mm (1/4 inch) potato inside each skin to form a shell. Fill the shells with the topping ingredients and bake as above.

1 Preheat the oven to 220°C (200°C fan/425°F).

2 Cut a large cross in the top of each Spud Man baked potato and gently squeeze the bottom to open up the top. Add a knob of butter and some salt and pepper. Place the potatoes on a baking tray.

3 Spoon some tomato sauce into each potato and divide the pepperoni and mushrooms or peppers among them. Roughly tear the mozzarella into pieces and scatter them over the top.

4 Bake in the oven for 12–15 minutes or until the mushrooms are cooked and golden brown and the mozzarella has melted. Drizzle with pesto and serve with a salad.

THE TOTALLY TROPICAL SPUD

When the sun is shining and I'm in a holiday mood, I start thinking about beaches and grilled chicken. Here's my recipe for succulent griddled chicken thighs with a sweet-and-spicy pineapple salsa (it works well with mango, too). It's also great if you cook the chicken over hot coals on the barbie – try it and see.

Serves 2 | Prep: 15 minutes | Cook: 15 minutes

2 x Spud Man baked potatoes

4 boneless chicken thighs, skin on

olive oil

2 large knobs of butter

4 tbsp sour cream

West Indian hot sauce

salt and freshly ground black pepper

Pineapple salsa

½ small pineapple

1 jalapeño or red bird's eye chilli, shredded or diced

½ red onion, diced

1 garlic clove, crushed

a small handful of chopped coriander

juice of 1 lime

olive oil

You can cook the chicken under an overhead grill or oven grill it if you don't have a grill pan.

1 Set a ridged grill pan over a medium to high heat and brush the chicken with a little olive oil and season with salt and pepper. When the pan is hot, place the chicken, skin-side down, on the grill and cook, pressing down with a spatula, for 5 minutes or so until the skin is golden brown and crisp. Turn the chicken over and cook for 8–10 minutes, or until it is cooked right through. You can pierce it with a sharp knife or skewer to check.

2 While the chicken is cooking, make the pineapple salsa: cut the end off the pineapple and remove the peel around the sides with a sharp knife. Cut into slices, removing the hard central core. Dice the juicy pineapple and transfer to a bowl with the chilli, red onion, garlic and coriander. Stir in the lime juice, a drizzle of olive oil and a pinch of salt.

3 Cut a large cross in the top of each Spud Man baked potato and gently squeeze the bottom to open up the top. Add a knob of butter and some salt and pepper.

4 Thinly slice the chicken thighs and add to the potatoes with the sour cream. Top with the pineapple salsa and drizzle with some West Indian hot sauce. Hot hot hot.

I WANT TO KEEP IT IN THE FAMILY

JULY

BBQ BONANZA

THE AMERICAN CLASSIC

4 July is American Independence Day and we're going to celebrate it in Spud Man style with these baked spuds loaded with chilli, cheese and jalapeños. You can make this chilli in advance and keep it in the fridge overnight before reheating, or you can freeze it.

Serves 2 | Prep: 15 minutes | Cook: 30–35 minutes

2 x Spud Man baked potatoes

2 large knobs of butter

4 heaped tbsp grated Cheddar cheese

2 bottled jalapeños, drained and sliced

a few dollops of sour cream

salt and freshly ground black pepper

Spicy salsa chilli

1 tbsp olive oil

1 onion, finely chopped

1 red pepper, deseeded and diced

2 garlic cloves, crushed

300g (10oz) lean minced beef

2 tsp chilli powder

120ml (4fl oz) beef stock

200g (7oz) fresh or bottled spicy tomato salsa

200g (7oz) tinned chopped tomatoes

200g (7oz) tinned kidney beans, drained

1 Make the spicy salsa chilli: heat the olive oil in a pan set over a low to medium heat and cook the onion, red pepper and garlic, stirring occasionally, for 6 minutes or until tender.

2 Stir in the mince and chilli powder and cook for 5 minutes, stirring, until browned all over. Add the stock, salsa, tomatoes and beans and cook gently for 15–20 minutes or until the sauce has thickened and the minced beef is cooked. Season with salt and pepper, to taste.

3 Cut a large cross in the top of each Spud Man baked potato and gently squeeze the bottom to open up the top. Add a knob of butter and some salt and pepper.

4 Place the potatoes in two bowls and spoon the chilli over the top. Sprinkle with cheese and jalapeños, add a dollop or two of sour cream and you're rockin'.

Hot Dog Spuds

If you don't have time to make the chilli, just cook some frankfurters on the grill and pop one into each buttery baked potato. Smother with grated mixed Cheddar and mozzarella and drizzle with ketchup and American mustard.

You can customize these spuds by stirring some sweetcorn into the chilli, adding a sprinkle of chopped coriander, or topping them with diced avocado or a spoonful of guacamole. Be adventurous!

SWEET & SPICY SEAFOOD SPUD

This summery spud is topped with juicy grilled prawns and a dollop of spicy fresh mango salsa. You can use fresh or frozen and defrosted raw tiger prawns, which will be ready to eat as soon as they turn from grey to pink. Alternatively, just reheat some cooked prawns in the oil and butter for 2–3 minutes each side.

Serves 2 | Prep: 15 minutes | Cook: 5 minutes

2 x Spud Man baked potatoes

1 tbsp olive oil

15g (½oz) butter

3 garlic cloves, crushed

a pinch of chilli flakes

250g (9oz) raw tiger prawns, shelled and deveined

sweet paprika

a few sprigs of parsley, chopped

2 large knobs of butter

salt and freshly ground black pepper

Mango salsa

1 ripe mango, peeled, stone removed and diced

½ red pepper, deseeded and diced

½ red onion, finely chopped

1 ripe tomato, chopped

1 jalapeño or other chilli, diced

a handful of chopped coriander

juice of 1 lime

1 Make the mango salsa: mix all the ingredients together in a bowl and add salt to taste. Set aside for the flavours to develop while you cook the prawns.

2 Heat the olive oil and butter in a large frying pan set over a medium to high heat. Add the garlic and chilli flakes and cook for 30 seconds, taking care not to brown the garlic. Add the prawns in a single layer and cook for 1–2 minutes until they are pink underneath. Turn them over and cook for 1–2 minutes on the other side or until pink and tender. Dust with the sweet paprika, season with salt and pepper and stir in the chopped parsley. Remove from the pan.

3 Cut a large cross in the top of each Spud Man baked potato and gently squeeze the bottom to open up the top. Add a knob of butter and some salt and pepper.

4 Place the potatoes in two bowls and top with the prawns and a very large dollop of mango salsa.

Don't overcook the prawns or they will go hard. Remove them from the pan as soon as they're pink on both sides and they'll be gorgeous, tender and succulent.

THE SEASIDE SPUD

These loaded spuds always make me think of great British seaside holidays eating fish and chips out of newspaper on the beach. I fill mine with cod bites and mushy peas, plus loads of tartare sauce. You can buy a jar in the supermarket or make it yourself. My recipe is quick and easy and it's The Real Thing! Over to you…

Serves 2 | Prep: 20 minutes | Cook: 15–20 minutes

2 x Spud Man baked potatoes

2 large knobs of butter

salt and freshly ground black pepper

Cod bites

400g (14oz) skinless thick cod fillet

plain flour

sweet paprika

2–3 tbsp olive oil

a few sprigs of parsley, chopped

200g (7oz) mushy peas (tinned or homemade)

Tartare sauce

1 egg

4 tbsp mayo

3 gherkins, diced

1 tbsp capers, diced

1 tbsp chopped parsley

a squeeze of lemon juice

1 Boil the egg for 8 minutes. Place in a bowl of cold water and set aside. When it's cold, peel and dice.

2 Make the tartare sauce: place all the ingredients in a bowl and stir until everything is well combined.

3 Make the cod bites: cut the cod into bite-sized pieces. Season with salt and pepper and dust with flour and paprika until lightly coated all over.

4 Heat the olive oil in a frying pan set over a medium to high heat. Add the cod and cook for 2–3 minutes until golden brown underneath. Turn the cod over and fry the other side until golden and cooked right through. Remove from the pan and drain on kitchen paper. Sprinkle with the parsley.

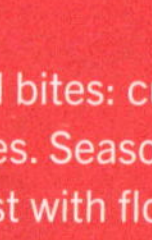

If you're in a hurry or don't have any fresh fish at home, you can cheat and use supermarket battered or breaded cod bites.

5 Cut a large cross in the top of each Spud Man baked potato and gently squeeze the bottom to open up the top. Add a knob of butter and some salt and pepper. Place the potatoes in two bowls.

6 Reheat the mushy peas in a pan on the hob (following the instructions on the tin) and divide among the potatoes. Top with the cod bites and loads of gorgeous tartare sauce. Spudelicious!

AUGUST

HOLIDAY VIBES

THIS IS PROBABLY THE EASIEST AND QUICKEST TOMATO SAUCE YOU'LL EVER MAKE. YOU CAN USE IT FOR PASTA, TOO – STIR IT INTO DRAINED SPAGHETTI OR LINGUINE AND SERVE SPRINKLED WITH LOADS OF GRATED PARMESAN

CAPRESE SKINS

Have you got friends coming over for drinks or are you throwing a small garden party or BBQ? Everyone will love these loaded skins – they're the equivalent of the classic Italian summer salad in a baked potato!

Serves 4 | Prep: 10 minutes | Cook: 17–20 minutes

4 x Spud Man baked potatoes

4 large knobs of butter, softened
2 garlic cloves, crushed
250g (9oz) mozzarella or 2 balls, drained
green pesto (optional)
a few basil leaves
salt and freshly ground black pepper

Quick smashed tomato sauce

3 tbsp olive oil
500g (1lb 2oz) cherry tomatoes
2 garlic cloves, crushed
a pinch of caster sugar

1 Make the quick smashed tomato sauce: heat the olive oil in a large frying pan set over a medium heat. Add the whole cherry tomatoes and garlic and cook, stirring occasionally, for 8–10 minutes or until the tomatoes burst. When they start to soften, press down on them with a spatula or wooden spoon to release their juice. Cook for 4–5 minutes more, or until the sauce reduces and thickens. Add the sugar and season with salt and pepper.

2 Meanwhile, cut the cooked Spud Man baked potatoes in half and spoon out the flesh, leaving about 5mm (¼ inch) potato inside each skin to form a shell. Season lightly with salt and pepper. (Keep the scooped-out potato for mashing and serving for another meal.)

3 Mix the softened butter with the crushed garlic and divide among the potato skins, then cover with the tomato sauce. Tear the mozzarella into pieces and scatter over the tomato sauce to fill the skins.

4 Pop the loaded skins under a preheated overhead grill or back into the oven for 5 minutes, or until the mozzarella melts. Drizzle with pesto, if using, and scatter the basil over the top.

YOU CAN MAKE YOUR OWN DELICIOUS CRISPY CROUTONS BY FRYING SOME BREAD CUBES IN THE LEFTOVER BACON FAT IN THE PAN

THE SUMMER CAESAR SALAD SPUD

Who doesn't like a chicken Caesar salad? Cheesy and garlicky with crisp lettuce and tender chicken in a creamy dressing, topped with crispy bacon and golden croûtons. This is the business... and it's so easy to make. The taste of summer in a spud.

Serves 2 | Prep: 15 minutes | Cook: 5 minutes

2 x Spud Man baked potatoes

2 large knobs of butter

salt and freshly ground black pepper

Caesar dressing

3 tbsp mayo

½ tsp Dijon mustard

grated zest and juice of 1 small lemon

2 garlic cloves, crushed

45g (1½oz) grated Parmesan

a few drops of Worcestershire sauce

Caesar salad topping

60g (2oz) bacon lardons or diced pancetta

a handful of shredded Cos or Little Gem lettuce

200g (7oz) cooked chicken, diced

crispy bread croûtons

2–3 tbsp grated Parmesan

1 Make the Caesar dressing: mix all the ingredients together in a large bowl, adding a few drops of Worcestershire sauce to taste.

2 Cut a large cross in the top of each Spud Man baked potato and gently squeeze the bottom to open up the top. Add a knob of butter and some salt and pepper. Place the potatoes in two bowls.

3 Make the Caesar salad topping: set a frying pan over a medium to high heat and, when it's hot, add the bacon or pancetta. Cook, turning occasionally, for 5 minutes, or until crisp and golden brown. Remove with a slotted spoon and drain on kitchen paper.

4 Gently toss the lettuce, chicken and croûtons in the Caesar dressing and spoon over the potatoes. Sprinkle the bacon and grated Parmesan over the top and serve immediately.

LOWES POTATOES
LOWES POTATOES
H Lowe & Sons

BANGIN' BRAZILIAN BEANS

Black beans served with rice are among the most popular Brazilian foods, but swapping the rice for my Spud Man baked potatoes transforms them into something really special. To make them swicy (sweet and spicy) and even more colourful, you can also use orange-fleshed sweet potatoes.

Serves 2 | Prep: 15 minutes | Cook: 20–25 minutes

2 x Spud Man baked potatoes

2 large knobs of butter

60g (2oz) grated Cheddar or Swiss cheese

salt and freshly ground black pepper

Brazilian beans topping

2 tbsp olive oil

1 onion, finely chopped

1 red or yellow pepper, deseeded and diced

1 red chilli, diced

3 garlic cloves, crushed

1 tsp smoked paprika

200g (7oz) tinned chopped tomatoes

200g (7oz) tinned black beans, rinsed and drained

You can turn up the heat and the spice by using hot chillies and adding some chilli powder and ground cumin.

1 Make the Brazilian beans topping: heat the olive oil in a pan set over a medium heat and cook the onion and pepper for 6–8 minutes, until softened. Stir in the chilli, garlic and smoked paprika and cook for 2–3 minutes.

2 Add the tomatoes and beans and continue cooking for 10 minutes, or until the vegetables are tender and the tomato sauce reduces and thickens. Season with salt and pepper.

3 Cut a large cross in the top of each Spud Man baked potato and gently squeeze the bottom to open up the top. Add a knob of butter and some salt and pepper. Place the potatoes in two bowls.

4 Spoon the Brazilian beans over the potatoes and sprinkle with the cheese. Pop under a preheated overhead grill until the cheese melts and bubbles. Don't hang about – eat immediately!

SEPTEMBER

BACK TO SCHOOL

You might just survive on spuds for the next three years. They're cheaper than kebabs

THE INDIAN SUMMER SPUD

For those of you who can't let go of the gap year and are finally starting college, here's a cheap and cheerful spud filled with spicy cauliflower florets and topped with sweet mango chutney. I just can't get enough of it.

Serves 2 | Prep: 15 minutes | Cook: 20–25 minutes

2 x Spud Man baked potatoes

2 large knobs of butter

2 heaped spoonfuls of mango chutney

2 dollops of Greek yoghurt

salt and freshly ground black pepper

Spice mix

1 tsp chilli powder

1 tsp garam masala

1 tsp ground coriander

½ tsp ground turmeric

Cauli aloo gobi topping

2 tbsp vegetable oil

1 small onion, finely chopped

½ tsp cumin seeds

2.5cm (1 inch) piece of ginger, peeled and grated

3 garlic cloves, crushed

1 tsp chilli flakes

250g (9oz) cauliflower florets, cut into smaller pieces

2 tomatoes, chopped

a small handful of chopped coriander

1 Make the spice mix: mix all the spices together in a small bowl.

2 Make the cauli aloo gobi topping: heat the oil in a pan set over a medium heat. Add the onion and cook, stirring occasionally, for 6–8 minutes or until tender and golden. Add the cumin seeds, ginger and garlic and cook for 1 minute. Stir in the chilli flakes and spice mix together with the cauliflower and cook for 3–4 minutes.

3 Sprinkle 3 tablespoons water over the top, reduce the heat to a simmer and cover the pan. Cook for a few more minutes until the cauliflower is tender but still has some bite.

4 Add the tomatoes and cook gently for 5 minutes, then stir in the chopped coriander. Check the seasoning.

5 Cut a large cross in the top of each Spud Man baked potato and gently squeeze the bottom to open up the top. Add a knob of butter and some salt and pepper. Place the potatoes in two bowls.

6 Spoon the cauli aloo gobi topping over the potatoes and top with the mango chutney and Greek yoghurt.

THE CUT-PRICE KEBAB SPUD

Don't order in an expensive takeout – my kebab spuds make a cheap and easy supper for college students embracing their new lifestyle on a budget. They're very versatile and you can substitute your favourite marinade or sauce and even add some chopped lettuce, tomatoes and cucumber.

Serves 2 | Prep: 15 minutes | Marinate: 15 minutes + Cook: 10–12 minutes

2 x Spud Man baked potatoes

2 large knobs of butter

2 garlic cloves, crushed

tzatziki or yoghurt

chilli sauce

salt and freshly ground black pepper

Chicken kebabs

4 skinless boneless chicken thighs

1 tbsp olive oil

a pinch of dried oregano

1 tsp sweet paprika

juice of ½ lemon

1 red onion, cut into wedges

1 red or yellow pepper, deseeded and cut into chunks

If using wooden skewers, soak them in water first to prevent them burning.

1 Make the chicken kebabs: cut the chicken thighs into bite-sized pieces and place in a bowl with the olive oil, oregano, paprika, lemon juice and some salt and pepper. Stir and leave to marinate for at least 15 minutes.

2 Thread the chicken, onion and pepper onto two kebab skewers and brush with any leftover marinade. Place them on a foil-lined grill pan and cook under a preheated overhead grill for 10–12 minutes, turning them occasionally, until the chicken is golden brown and cooked right through.

3 Meanwhile, cut a large cross in the top of each Spud Man baked potato and gently squeeze the bottom to open up the top. Add a knob of butter, the garlic and some salt and pepper, and mash gently into the potato.

4 Transfer the potatoes to two plates and top each one with a chicken kebab. You can take the chicken and vegetables off the skewers, if you fancy. Top with tzatziki or yoghurt and drizzle with chilli sauce.

SLOPPY JOES STUDY BUDDY SPUD

It's back to school time and there are always some late-night study sessions when you need more than just a snack to keep you going. If you're feeling peckish, here are my tasty sloppy Joes to get you focused and back on track.

Serves 2 | Prep: 15 minutes | Cook: 30–35 minutes

2 x Spud Man baked potatoes

2 large knobs of butter

crispy fried onions

grated Cheddar cheese

salt and freshly ground black pepper

Speedy mince topping

1 tbsp olive oil

1 small onion, finely chopped

½ red or yellow pepper, deseeded and chopped

2 garlic cloves, crushed

250g (9oz) minced beef

1 tbsp tomato paste

200g (7oz) tinned chopped tomatoes

120g (4oz) tomato ketchup

½ tsp mustard

1 tsp light brown sugar

a dash of Worcestershire sauce

1 Make the speedy mince topping: heat the oil in a saucepan set over a medium heat and cook the onion and pepper, stirring occasionally, for 6–8 minutes until tender. Stir in the garlic and cook for 2 minutes.

2 Add the minced beef, breaking it up with a wooden spoon, and cook, stirring, until browned all over. Stir in the remaining ingredients and continue cooking for 15–20 minutes, or until the sauce thickens and reduces. Check the seasoning, adding salt and pepper to taste.

3 Meanwhile, cut a large cross in the top of each Spud Man baked potato and gently squeeze the bottom to open up the top. Add a knob of butter and some salt and pepper and place the potatoes in two bowls.

4 Pour the speedy mince over the potatoes and sprinkle with lots of crispy onions and Cheddar.

You can spice up the sloppy Joes by adding some chilli powder or chilli sauce to the minced beef.

OCTOBER

SPOOKY SPUDS

HARVEST FESTIVAL SPUD

At this time of year, root vegetables come into their own and make a sweetly caramelized and crispy topping for baked spuds. I use carrots, parsnips, beetroot and shallots, but swede and red onions also work well. Vegans can substitute maple syrup for the honey and use dairy-free tzatziki or cheese.

Serves 2 | Prep: 15 minutes | Cook: 45 minutes

2 x Spud Man baked potatoes

2 large knobs of butter

tzatziki or grated Cheddar or Swiss cheese

salt and freshly ground black pepper

Roasted roots topping

2 carrots, peeled and cut into thin sticks

1 parsnip, peeled and cut lengthways into quarters and then in half

1 small beetroot, peeled and cut into small chunks

3 shallots, peeled and halved (or small red onion wedges)

3 garlic cloves in their skins

olive oil

balsamic vinegar or glaze

2–3 tsp runny honey

a few sprigs of flat-leaf parsley, chopped

1 Make the roasted roots topping: preheat the oven to 180°C (160°C fan/350°F).

2 Spread out the vegetables on a large baking tray, tucking the garlic cloves in between. Drizzle with plenty of olive oil and a little balsamic vinegar or glaze, plus the honey. Season lightly with salt and pepper. Roast in the oven for 45 minutes, or until the vegetables are tender and starting to crisp. Squeeze the garlic out of their skins and mix with the vegetables. Stir in the parsley.

3 Cut a large cross in the top of each Spud Man baked potato and gently squeeze the bottom to open up the top. Add a knob of butter and some salt and pepper and place the potatoes in two bowls.

4 Spoon the roasted vegetables over the potatoes and top with some tzatziki or loads of grated cheese.

Don't cut the vegetables too thick or too large. The smaller and thinner they are the crispier they'll be – more tender, too.

THE GHOSTLY GARLIC SPUD

If you're a big fan of garlic like me, you'll love my special ghostly garlic spud – it will take your breath away and scare literally everyone around you too. Back in the day, people often hung garlic bulbs above the front door to frighten away evil spirits, so this is the perfect spud for Halloween.

Serves 2 | Prep: 15 minutes | Cook: 40–45 minutes

2 x Spud Man baked potatoes

2 small knobs of butter
5 heaped tbsp cream cheese
grated Parmesan (optional)
a few dollops of sour cream (optional)
salt and freshly ground black pepper

Creamy garlicky filling

1 whole garlic bulb in its skin
2 tsp olive oil
85g (3oz) butter, melted
a few chives, chopped

1 Preheat the oven to 200°C (180°C fan/400°F).

2 Make the creamy garlicky filling: slice the top off the garlic bulb and discard any papery outer layers. Place on a square of foil and drizzle with the olive oil. Bring the four corners of the foil up and over the garlic and twist at the top to seal the package. Place on a baking tray and roast in the oven for 40–45 minutes. The garlic should be soft and golden brown.

3 When the garlic is cool enough to handle, squeeze the base to push the softened garlic out of their skins and mash it with a fork. Stir into the melted butter together with the chives.

4 Cut a large cross in the top of each Spud Man baked potato and gently squeeze the bottom to open up the top. Mash in a knob of butter, some salt and pepper and the cream cheese.

5 Transfer to two bowls and pour the melted garlic butter over the top. For extra flavour and creaminess, top with some grated Parmesan and a dollop of sour cream. The aroma is heavenly if you're a garlic lover! Dig in and everyone will give you a wide berth for the next few hours. Only joking...

You can roast the garlic alongside the baked potatoes.

SLOW-COOKER CHINESE CHICKEN CURRY

Before you go out trick-or-treating for Halloween on a cold night, warm up with this tasty Chinese chicken curry. It couldn't be easier if you have a slow cooker – just leave it to cook for a few hours and pour over your baked spuds. Top with grated cheese and crispy fried onions and hey presto… no need to order one in from your local Chinese restaurant or takeaway.

Serves 2 | Prep: 10 minutes | Cook: 5½ hours

2 x Spud Man baked potatoes

2 large knobs of butter

60g (2oz) grated cheese, e.g. mixed Cheddar and mozzarella (see page 26)

loads of crispy fried onions

salt and freshly ground black pepper

Chinese chicken curry

2 chicken breasts, skinless and cut into cubes

1 small onion, finely chopped

½ red or green pepper, deseeded and diced

2 garlic cloves, crushed

2 tsp curry powder

1 tsp ground turmeric

1 tsp grated fresh ginger

a pinch of sugar

350ml (12fl oz) chicken stock

2 tsp soy sauce

3 tsp cornflour

4 tbsp frozen peas

1 Make the Chinese chicken curry: place the chicken, onion, pepper, garlic, curry powder, turmeric, ginger and sugar in the slow cooker. Add the stock and soy sauce and give it a good stir. Cook on low power for 5 hours.

2 Mix the cornflour with a little water until dissolved and smooth. Add to the chicken curry and stir until smooth. Add the peas and then cover the slow cooker and cook for a further 20 minutes.

3 Cut a large cross in the top of each Spud Man baked potato and gently squeeze the bottom to open up the top. Add a knob of butter and some salt and pepper and place the potatoes in two bowls.

4 Spoon the curry over the top and sprinkle with the grated cheese and crispy fried onions.

This is quite a mild curry, but you can make it hotter by adding fresh chillies or some chilli flakes.

THE MONSTER MASH

How about some spooky spuds topped with scary faces for Halloween? It's not only your little monsters who'll love them – mums and dads also get excited! They're fun to make and great to get you in the mood before you go out trick-or-treating. Tap into your creativity!

Serves 2 | Prep: 15 minutes | Cook: 8–10 minutes

2 x Spud Man baked potatoes

2 large knobs of butter

2 tbsp milk

60g (2oz) grated Cheddar cheese

2 spring onions, thinly sliced

salt and freshly ground black pepper

Monster mash topping

4 tbsp tomato pasta sauce (tinned, bottled or homemade)

100g (3½oz) shredded mozzarella or 1 ball, drained

sliced pimento-stuffed green olives or small pepperoni circles with pieces of black olive in the middle, for the eyes

sliced black olives, capers or red pepper triangles, for the noses

sliced red pepper or pepperoni, for the mouths (lips)

green pepper triangles or red or green bird's eye chillies, for the teeth

1 Preheat the oven to 200°C (180°C fan/400°F).

2 Cut the cooked Spud Man baked potatoes in half and spoon out the flesh, leaving about 5mm (¼ inch) potato inside each skin to form a shell.

3 Mash the scooped-out potato with the butter and milk and season with salt and pepper. Mix in the cheese and spring onions and replace in the shells, smoothing and levelling the top.

4 Make the monster mash topping: spread a spoonful of tomato pasta sauce over each potato half and cover with the shredded mozzarella. Alternatively, you can use slices of mozzarella cut to fit the shape of the potato up to the edges. You want the top to be as flat as possible.

5 Now make the monster faces on top. Use the pimento-stuffed green olive slices or small pepperoni circles with pieces of black olive in the middle for the pupils to make the eyes. Then add sliced black olives, capers or red pepper triangles for the noses and sliced red pepper or pepperoni for the lips. Finally, arrange green pepper triangles or bird's eye chillies for the teeth. Be adventurous!

6 Place the potatoes on a baking tray and bake in the oven for 8–10 minutes, or until the cheese melts. Transfer to serving plates and enjoy!

IF YOU'RE IN THE MOOD AND FEELING REALLY CREATIVE, YOU CAN DRIZZLE WITH SOME BEETROOT JUICE OR TOMATO KETCHUP FOR BLOOD

NOVEMBER

THE VEGGIE CHANA DAL SPUD

These fragrant, spicy spuds will warm you up on a cold Bonfire Night. The dal is easy to make and you can even cook it in advance to reheat later. I serve mine with a dollop of sweet fruity chutney and a sprinkle of coconut flakes. Vegans can use plant-based butter.

Serves 2 | Soak: 2–3 hours | Prep: 10 minutes | Cook: 35–50 minutes

2 x Spud Man baked potatoes

2 large knobs of butter

2 dollops of mango chutney

toasted coconut flakes

chopped coriander

salt and freshly ground black pepper

Chana dal topping

125g (4½oz) chana dal (split yellow chickpeas)

½ tsp ground turmeric

200ml (7fl oz) coconut milk

1 tbsp mustard oil (or vegetable oil)

1 large onion, thinly sliced

½ tsp cumin seeds

1 tsp ginger paste

1 bird's eye chilli, diced, or 1 tsp chilli powder

2 garlic cloves, crushed

1 tomato, chopped

Seasoning

1 tbsp mustard oil (or vegetable oil)

1 tsp mustard seeds

1 tsp black onion seeds

1–2 dried red chillies (depending on how much heat you like)

FEASTING SEASON

1 Make the chana dal topping: rinse the chana dal and tip into a bowl. Cover with water and set aside to soak for 2–3 hours. Drain well.

2 Transfer the chana dal to a saucepan and add the turmeric, coconut milk and 300ml (½ pint) water. Set over a high heat and bring to the boil, then lower the heat to a gentle simmer and cook for 30–40 minutes, or until the dal is tender.

3 While the dal is cooking, heat the oil in a frying pan set over a medium heat and cook the onion, stirring occasionally, for 8 minutes or so, until golden brown. Stir in the cumin seeds, ginger paste, chilli or chilli powder and garlic and cook for 1–2 minutes.

4 Stir the onion mixture and chopped tomato into the cooked dal and simmer for 5–10 minutes.

5 Meanwhile, make the seasoning: heat the oil in a pan set over a low to medium heat. Add the mustard and onion seeds and chillies and cook until the mustard seeds start to pop. Discard the chillies and stir the oil into the dal.

6 Cut a large cross in the top of each Spud Man baked potato and gently squeeze the bottom to open up the top. Add a knob of butter and some salt and pepper and place the potatoes in two bowls.

7 Spoon the dal over the potatoes and add a dollop of chutney. Sprinkle with toasted coconut flakes and coriander. Spicy!!

If you're not using mustard oil, stir ½–1 teaspoon English mustard into the dal at the end. Or use ghee for frying the onion.

If you don't have a slow cooker, use a casserole dish on the hob and then bake in the oven at 200°C (180°C fan/400°F).

BONFIRE NIGHT BANGERS

My favourite spuds for Guy Fawkes night – 5 November. You can make the spicy sausage stew in advance and leave it in the slow cooker. If you're having friends round, just double or triple the quantities – it's great for kids as well as mums and dads.

Serves 2 | Prep: 15 minutes | Cook: 2¾–3¼ hours

2 x Spud Man baked potatoes

2 large knobs of butter

grated Cheddar cheese

a few sprigs of flat-leaf parsley, chopped

salt and freshly ground black pepper

Slow-cooker sausage stew

1 tbsp olive oil

4 fat meaty pork sausages, e.g. Cumberland

1 red onion, chopped

1 red pepper, deseeded and diced

2 large carrots, chopped

1 garlic clove, crushed

1 red chilli, diced

1 tsp smoked paprika

a pinch of sugar

1 tbsp tomato ketchup

1 x 400g (14oz) tin of chopped tomatoes

400ml (14fl oz) chicken stock

2 tbsp cornflour

1 Make the slow-cooker sausage stew: heat the oil in a frying pan set over a medium to high heat and cook the sausages, turning occasionally, for 6–8 minutes, until browned all over. Transfer to a slow cooker.

2 Cook the onion, red pepper, carrot, garlic and chilli in the frying pan for 5 minutes. Stir in the paprika and sugar and add to the slow cooker together with the ketchup, tomatoes and stock. Cover and cook on high for 2½–3 hours.

3 Mix the cornflour with a little water until dissolved and smooth. Stir into the sausage stew and cook for a further 5–10 minutes until thickened. Check the seasoning.

4 Cut a large cross in the top of each Spud Man baked potato and gently squeeze the bottom to open up the top. Add a knob of butter and some salt and pepper and place the potatoes in two bowls.

5 Spoon the sausage stew over the top (if you wish, you can cut the sausages into quarters) and sprinkle with the Cheddar and parsley.

THANKSGIVING SPUDS

For a special Thanksgiving celebration, make my baked sweet potato spuds filled with turkey, stuffing and corn, and deluged with tasty gravy and fruity cranberry sauce. They're a feast in a bowl! You can also use leftover turkey and stuffing to fill and top the spuds.

Serves 2 | Prep: 15 minutes
Cook: 35–45 minutes

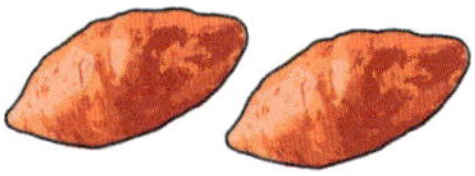

2 x Spud Man baked sweet potatoes (see tip)

2 large knobs of butter, softened

1–2 tbsp milk

4 thick slices of roast turkey, chopped

2 tbsp tinned sweetcorn, warmed

Onion Gravy (see page 33)

2 big dollops of cranberry sauce

salt and freshly ground black pepper

Thanksgiving stuffing

75g (2½oz) butter, plus extra for greasing

1 small leek, trimmed and thinly sliced

2 celery sticks, chopped

2 garlic cloves, crushed

250g (9oz) stale white bread (½ small crusty loaf), torn into pieces

a few sage leaves, chopped

1 tsp thyme leaves

a handful of chopped parsley

350–400ml (12–14fl oz) chicken stock

1 large egg, beaten

1 Make the Thanksgiving stuffing: preheat the oven to 180°C (160°C fan/350°F). Butter a small baking dish.

2 Melt the butter in a frying pan set over a low to medium heat and set aside 1 tablespoon. Add the leek, celery and garlic and cook, stirring occasionally, for 5 minutes. Transfer to a bowl and add the bread pieces and herbs. Mix until everything is coated in the butter. Add 350ml (12fl oz) of the chicken stock and the beaten egg and stir well. Season with salt and pepper. If the mixture is still a little on the dry side, add some more stock.

3 Spoon into the buttered baking dish and drizzle the remaining butter over the top. Cover with foil and bake in the oven for 25–30 minutes. Remove the foil and cook for a further 5–10 minutes until crisp and golden on top.

4 Cut a large cross in the top of each Spud Man sweet potato and gently squeeze the bottom to open up the top. Scoop out some of the cooked potato inside and mash it with the butter and milk. Stir in the turkey and sweetcorn and season to taste. Spoon back into the potatoes.

5 Place the potatoes in two shallow bowls and top with some pieces of crispy stuffing. Pour the gravy over them and serve with the cranberry sauce.

To roast sweet potatoes, wash and dry the potatoes, then rub them all over with a little oil. Sprinkle with salt and cook in a preheated oven at 200°C (180°C fan/400°F) for 45–60 minutes, or until tender when you squeeze them.

COMFORT CHICKEN CASSEROLE

It's so comforting and relaxing on a dark November night to treat yourself to one of my baked spuds topped with creamy chicken, mushrooms and bacon. This casserole is easy to assemble and you can make it in advance and reheat it later on, or even the next day. The perfect pick-me-up.

Serves 2 | Prep: 15 minutes | Cook: 1¼ hours

2 x Spud Man baked potatoes

2 large knobs of butter

salt and freshly ground black pepper

Chicken casserole

300g (10oz) skinless boneless chicken thighs, cut into large chunks

1 tbsp plain flour, plus extra for dusting

2 tbsp olive oil

1 small onion, finely chopped

1 small leek, trimmed and thinly sliced

115g (4oz) button mushrooms, sliced

60g (2oz) bacon lardons

300ml (10fl oz) chicken stock

a handful of frozen peas

2–3 tbsp crème fraîche

2 handfuls of chopped parsley

You can use chicken breast instead of thighs, but the flavour will be milder and less 'chickeny'.

1 Preheat the oven to 190°C (170°C fan/375°F).

2 Make the chicken casserole: dust the chicken thighs with flour. Heat the oil in a casserole dish set over a medium heat and cook the chicken, turning occasionally, for 6–8 minutes or until browned all over. Remove and set aside.

3 Add the onion, leek, mushrooms and bacon, and cook for 5 minutes, stirring occasionally, until golden brown. Stir in the flour and then add the stock, stirring well.

4 Add the chicken and then cover the casserole with a lid and cook in the oven for 45 minutes. Add the peas to the casserole and cook for a further 10 minutes, or until the sauce has thickened slightly. Stir in the crème fraîche and some of the parsley and check the seasoning.

5 Cut a large cross in the top of each Spud Man baked potato and gently squeeze the bottom to open up the top. Add a knob of butter and some salt and pepper and place the potatoes in two bowls. Spoon the chicken casserole over the top, sprinkle with the remaining parsley and enjoy!

DECEMBER

THE SPUDTASTIC WINTER WARMER

There's nothing more warming on a cold winter's night than a hearty, rich beef stew. I like to cook mine for several hours in the slow cooker to bring out all those lovely flavours and then spoon it over. Spudtastic!

Serves 2 | Soak: 2–3 hours | Prep: 15 minutes
Cook: 3¾–4¼ hours on high or 8¼ hours on low

2 x Spud Man baked potatoes

2 large knobs of butter
a handful of chopped parsley
salt and freshly ground black pepper

Beef stew

2 tbsp olive oil
1 small onion, chopped
1 celery stick, chopped
1 carrot, sliced
1 parsnip, sliced
2 garlic cloves, crushed
2 tbsp tomato paste
a few glugs of red wine (optional)
350ml (12fl oz) hot beef stock
a few shakes of Worcestershire sauce
1 bay leaf
3 sprigs of thyme
a thin strip of orange peel
300g (10oz) stewing or braising beef, cut into chunks
plain flour

FESTIVE FEASTS

1 Heat the oil in a large deep frying pan set over a low heat and cook the onion, celery and carrot for 6–8 minutes, until just softened. Add the parsnip and garlic and cook for 2 minutes.

2 Remove with a slotted spoon and transfer to a slow cooker. Stir in the tomato paste and add the wine, if using, stock, Worcestershire sauce, herbs and orange peel.

3 Toss the beef in some flour until lightly coated. Add to the frying pan and cook, stirring occasionally, for 3–4 minutes or until browned all over. Transfer to the slow cooker and grind in a little black pepper.

4 Cover and cook on high for 3½–4 hours or on low for 8 hours. Check the seasoning, adding salt and pepper, if needed.

5 Cut a large cross in the top of each Spud Man baked potato and gently squeeze the bottom to open up the top. Add a knob of butter and some salt and pepper and place the potatoes in two bowls. Spoon the beef stew over the top, sprinkle with parsley and enjoy!

If at the end the stew is not thick enough for your liking, mix 1 tablespoon cornflour and a little cold water together until smooth. Stir into the stew and cook for 10–15 minutes until thickened.

If you don't have a slow cooker, use a casserole dish on top of the hob and then cook, covered, in a preheated oven at 170°C (150°C fan/325°F) for 2 hours. Remove the lid and cook for another 30 minutes or so until the sauce has thickened and the beef is tender.

PARTY PLATTER MINI SPUDS

These festive mini spuds are the perfect seasonal treats or canapés for sharing at Christmas parties and buffets. You can bake the potatoes earlier in the day and reheat them just before serving (it's ok, just this once). This is the ultimate festive feast.

Makes 24 | Prep: 20 minutes | Cook: 50–65 minutes

24 small baby or new potatoes
olive oil
sea salt flakes
24 small knobs of butter
sour cream (optional)
salt and freshly ground black pepper

Pigs in blankets topping

8 pork chipolata or cocktail sausages
8 streaky bacon rashers
1 tsp wholegrain mustard
2 tsp runny honey

Devils on horseback topping

4 streaky bacon rashers, cut in half
8 soft prunes

Cranberry cheesy melt topping

85g (3oz) Brie or Camembert, cut into 8 thin slices
60g (2oz) cranberry sauce
grated zest and juice of 1 clementine

1 Preheat the oven to 200°C (180°C fan/400°F). Rub the potatoes all over with olive oil and place them on a baking tray. Sprinkle the sea salt flakes over the top. Bake in the oven for 45–55 minutes, or until golden brown and softened when you squeeze them. While they are cooking, make the toppings.

2 Make the pigs in blankets: wrap each sausage in a rasher of bacon and place on a foil-lined baking tray. Heat the mustard and honey in a small pan set over a low heat and brush over the bacon-wrapped sausages. Bake in the oven for 15–20 minutes.

3 Make the devils on horseback: stretch each piece of streaky bacon with a thin-bladed knife until it's longer and thinner. Wrap each one around a prune and secure with a wooden toothpick or cocktail stick. Place them on a baking tray and brush lightly with olive oil. Bake in the oven for 10 minutes, or until the bacon is golden brown and crispy.

4 When the potatoes are cooked, cut a cross in the top of each one and gently squeeze the bottom to open up the top. Add a knob of butter and some salt and

pepper. Top eight of them with the pigs in blankets and eight with the devils on horseback (removing the toothpicks). Keep warm.

5 Make the cranberry cheesy melt topping: push a slice of cheese inside each of the remaining eight potatoes. Mix the cranberry sauce with the clementine zest and juice and add a small dollop to each potato. Place on a baking tray and bake in the oven for 5–10 minutes until the cheese melts.

6 Serve immediately with a bowl of sour cream on the side. These are finger lickin' good.

You can cook the pigs in blankets and devils on horseback on the oven shelf underneath the potatoes.

CHRISTMAS DINNER SPUD

My humongous Christmas spuds are oozing with melted cheese and filled with crispy bacon, roast turkey and stuffing. I like to eat them with big dollops of cranberry sauce and loads of gravy. They are very versatile and a great way of using up leftovers on Boxing Day, too – try mixing in some chipolata sausages, cooked sprouts and chestnuts.

Serves 2 | Prep: 15 minutes | Cook: 9–16 minutes

2 x Spud Man baked potatoes

2 large knobs of butter, softened

1–2 tbsp milk

salt and freshly ground black pepper

Christmas dinner topping

4 streaky bacon rashers

4 thick slices of roast turkey, chopped

60g (2oz) grated mixed Cheddar and mozzarella (see page 26)

100g (3½oz) sage and onion stuffing, cut into chunks

2 big dollops of cranberry sauce

Onion Gravy (see page 33)

You can use homemade, shop-boughtor made-up packet stuffing, whatever's easier.

1 Cook the bacon in a frying pan set over a medium to high heat for 2–3 minutes until golden brown underneath. Flip the bacon over and cook the other side until crispy and golden. Remove and drain on kitchen paper.

2 Cut a large cross in the top of each Spud Man baked potato and gently squeeze the bottom to open up the top. Scoop out most of the cooked potato inside and mash it with the butter and milk. Crumble the bacon over the top and mix it in with the turkey and grated cheese. Spoon it back into the potato shells and top with the stuffing and cranberry sauce.

3 Place on a baking tray and pop back into the oven (in which you baked the potatoes) or place under a hot overhead grill for 5–10 minutes. Divide between two bowls and pour the gravy over the top.

MERRY
CHRISTMAS!

GIVE THE GIFT OF SPUDS

THIS CHRISTMAS

VEGGIE CHRISTMAS DAY SPUD

This is a great way for all you vegetarians out there to enjoy a traditional Christmas dinner. Make it easy and delicious by stuffing and topping my famous baked spuds with all the festive foods and flavours. If you're a vegan, you don't have to miss out – you can do vegan butter, plant milk and cheese swaps.

Serves 2 | Prep: 15 minutes | Cook: 35–45 minutes

2 x Spud Man baked potatoes

2 large knobs of butter, softened

1–2 tbsp milk

salt and freshly ground black pepper

1 large carrot, sliced, boiled, drained and mashed

6 cooked Brussels sprouts, drained and shredded

45g (1½oz) vegetarian Stilton, crumbled

Onion Gravy (see page 33 and use vegan Worcester sauce)

cranberry sauce (optional)

stuffing (optional)

Caramelized fried onions

15g (½oz) unsalted butter

1 tbsp olive oil

1 large onion, thinly sliced

2 garlic cloves, crushed

2 tsp red wine vinegar

4 tsp light brown sugar

1 Make the caramelized fried onions: heat the butter and olive oil in a frying pan set over a low heat. Add the sliced onions and cook very slowly and gently for 30–40 minutes, stirring occasionally, until tender, golden brown and starting to caramelize. Watch carefully in case they burn. Add the garlic and cook for 1 minute, then stir in the vinegar and sugar. Cook gently for 5 minutes, stirring until the sugar dissolves.

2 Cut a large cross in the top of each Spud Man baked potato and gently squeeze the bottom to open up the top. Scoop out most of the cooked potato inside and mash it with the butter and milk. Mix with the mashed carrot, shredded sprouts and Stilton. Season with salt and pepper to taste.

3 Spoon the mixture into the potato shells, pressing it down firmly, and put the potatoes in two bowls. Top with the caramelized onions and drizzle the gravy over the top. Serve immediately with some cranberry sauce and stuffing, if using, on the side.

Add a little crunch with chopped toasted hazelnuts or walnuts. Go on, treat yourself ... it's Christmas!

QUICK–FIRE SPUDS

Mash or roasties?
Roasties. Easy.

Skin on or skin off roasties?
Skin off.

Butter or olive oil?
Butter.

Chunky chips or fries?
Chunky chips.

Floury or waxy?
Floury, I think.

Grow your own or trust a farmer?
I like growing my own, but every time there's a heat wave and I go off for the weekend, SpudWife doesn't water my potatoes and they all die. So, trust a farmer, because when you come back from Wrexham your potatoes aren't... dead.

Air fryer or proper oven?
I'm not even answering that one.

Fight a man-sized potato or be chased by a swarm of 1,000 small potatoes?
How fast is this swarm of small potatoes? Does the man-sized potato have man-sized legs? I think the small potatoes. I think you could just stamp on them. And what damage are they going to do? Unless they like combine into like a mega potato.

Live the rest of your life only eating potatoes or never eat potato again?
So, I can have every other food in the world and no potatoes or just potatoes? I ******* love potatoes but I would lose my mind in about two weeks if I just ate potato. Potato for breakfast, potato for lunch, potato for dinner? I would go mad. I'm going to go every other food. However much I love potatoes, that's a no-brainer.

ACKNOWLEDGEMENTS

To Sarah and the kids: I love you more than taters.

To Grandad Bernard, thanks for many hours of adventures on the farm growing up. You passed away at the age of 98 but even in those last few days, you still wanted to make sure business was going well. I know you would have been proud to see this second book. Hope you're enjoying the apple juice with Grandma and my dad. Love you always.

To Grandma Joan, still the best maker of pancakes in the world – I miss you each day and know you would be so proud of me.

To my dad, Michael, potato merchant to many! Dad who would have loved every second of all that has happened. Always there to help, even when you yourself were not well. I miss you.

To Gaz and Seddon and their families, thanks for a lifetime of friendship and memories – and here's to many more years to come, even if we're older and greyer (or balder).

And to the renal team at the Royal Derby, and particularly the home dialysis team, without whom I couldn't do any of what I do. Here's to you Berrnan Rivera, Carol Rhodes, Chris Swan, Geoff Inacay and Dr Richard Fluck.

SPUD MAN'S
SPUDS
FOR ALL
SEASONS